'Jane is a realist, a generous encourager, a determined follower of Jesus, and a fellow creative. Please read and use this book.'
Bridget Plass, writer and speaker

'The prayers in this book are considered, wise, and beautiful. Using them will help artisans of every kind offer our work and creative play up to the living God who takes joy in our efforts.'
Keren Dibbens-Wyatt, Christian contemplative and creative

'A tender and luminous guide for anyone who creates with heart and faith. This book is both a prayer and a practice, a companion for those who long to make creativity – and life itself – an act of worship.'
Cathy Edge RSM, @KnittingNun

'*Bless the Work of Our Hands* is a sensitively written feast of prayers. Jane has written an honest and very down-to-earth book that will resonate strongly with professional and amateur creatives alike.'
Mary Fleeson, artist and writer, lindisfarne-scriptorium.co.uk

'Thanksgiving spills from the pages, with a treasure trove of uplifting prayers. This beautiful book is achingly honest, with deeply personal stories shared that give voice to the cries of joy, failure, or inertia that will certainly resonate.'
Claire Daniel, author and speaker

'All creatives should have a copy of this beautiful book at their elbow! What an inspiring gift for any writer, crafter or musician to be connected in prayer and imagination with our creator God.'
Amy Scott Robinson, author and performance storyteller

BRF Ministries

15 The Chambers, Vineyard
Abingdon OX14 3FE
+44(0)1865 319700 | brf.org.uk

Bible Reading Fellowship (BRF) is a charity (233280) and company limited by
guarantee (301324), registered in England and Wales

EU Authorised Representative: Easy Access System Europe – Mustamäe tee 50,
10621 Tallinn, Estonia, **gpsr.requests@easproject.com**

ISBN 978 1 80039 418 6
First published 2026
All rights reserved

Prayers &
reflections for creatives

BLESS THE WORK
OF OUR HANDS

Written & illustrated
by Jane Walters

BRF
Ministries

Contents

Introduction

Christian creative.

That's me, and I guess that it's you, too.

It's a wonderful privilege to partner with our creator God! I have loved making things throughout my life. I was going to add 'in good times and bad' but, of course, being creative is what can turn bad times around. Whether we're thinking of a crafted physical object, of music or of hand-picked words, each can be tools in God's hands to bring comfort, convey love, and lift the eye above the drabness of the mundane.

It's not just about the finished product, though. (I avert my eyes gratefully from the massive pile of half-started items.) Being creative is the time/space where we are left to our own thoughts and devices, where we can work and play to our heart and soul's content and satisfaction; and, yes, the place where we can make mess and mistakes, too.

Creativity is a wonderful expression of the gospel. Although God created us perfect, we were soon marred by sin and have been part of a re-creation process ever since. The act of creativity is rarely a 'once-and-for-all' event, but a process, an unfolding, a re-working. As Christian creatives, we must never lose sight of this living metaphor of God's work in us.

Please note my use of the phrase 'work-play' to describe our activity. Some of us are hobbyists, others are full-time creative professionals, but each of us performs the tasks of our craft as earnestly as if we were working, and as light-spirited as if we were playing.

How to use this book

These prayers and reflections offer the opportunity to dedicate ourselves and our activities to God, in humble recognition that he is the source of all inspiration, the one who gives wisdom at every stage and the sustainer who can get us to the end goal.

There are scripture references throughout, to help ground our thinking and praying in his word. It is a key component of this book, so don't be tempted to skip over the verses. It is my experience that my best times of creativity have come out of my dedicated times with God.

Inevitably there are drawbacks to a resource like this. The way I speak to God will not precisely match yours. The words I use may miss the mark for you. But it is my hope and prayer that something of the heart behind and within them will resonate with yours. By all means, modify the wording, add your own lines – whatever it takes to make this book personal to you.

The sections can be dipped in and out of according to need – and, of course, you are free to borrow prayers from a different craft! The longer reflections and poems are designed to provoke your own thinking.

My fervent prayer would be that you find fresh ways of engaging with our creator God; that you would meet him as you work-play and discover more of why you were created in the first place.

1

PRAYERS OF THANKSGIVING AND WORSHIP

I will praise God's name in song and glorify him with thanksgiving.
PSALM 69:30

Do not be anxious about anything, but in every situation, by prayer and petition, with thanksgiving, present your requests to God.
PHILIPPIANS 4:6

The Son is the image of the invisible God, the firstborn over all creation. For in him all things were created: things in heaven and on earth, visible and invisible, whether thrones or powers or rulers or authorities; all things have been created through him and for him.
COLOSSIANS 1:15–16

God, I want to thank you for creativity,
  for the grace-filled gift it is
  to partake in your nature!
You could have reserved this privilege and pleasure for
    yourself,
  but instead you shared it freely
  among all of humankind,
  allowing my space here
  to become a piece of heaven.
God, thank you for calling me to be a creative.
Thank you for gifting me with talents
  and granting opportunities to explore them.
I consider myself beyond blessed,
  overwhelmed at this lavish demonstration
  of your goodness.
Thank you for what creating does to my inner being:
  exciting my mind with wonder and possibility;
  soothing my soul with peace and lifting my cares;
  satisfying my heart with deep contentment.
My words of praise may falter and fail,
  but receive this thanksgiving
  from a grateful heart, I pray.
Amen.

———

God, I thank you for the gift of a new day.
Thank you that your word promises
  your mercies are new every morning
  and great is your faithfulness.
Thank you that yesterday,
  with all its trials and testing,
  is behind me.
Today I have new opportunities,
  new strength,
    fresh inspiration,
      living hope.
Thank you, God, that I don't rely on yesterday's crumbs
  but feast on today's daily bread.
May you be my helper today,
  my cheerleader,
  the faithful one who will take my hand and not let go.
Perfect, holy God,
  accept these imperfect offerings
  of me and what I create.
Amen.

———

God, I am surrounded by other voices
  clamouring for my attention, but –
  most insidious of all –
  claiming to be the source of all I need.
So I come to you today,
  not as the Universe,
  nor as Supreme Power,
    though those titles are true of you.
I come in full acknowledgement
  that you are the only true God,
  shown to us in flesh as Jesus Christ,
  your Word incarnate.
When I pray today,
  it is to you,
    God Almighty,
      El Shaddai.
You are the all-sufficient one,
  the Jehovah Jireh who meets every need.
You are El Roi,
  the God who sees –
  and not only sees, but knows
  and, what is more,
  comes gloriously to our aid.
Let all I do today be inspired by you.
Let all I do today bring glory to you.
Let nothing detract from who you are.
There is a God:
  and it's not me,
  nor anything or anyone else.
Hallelujah!
Amen.

———

God, I worship you as creator,
  initiator and sustainer,
  thanking you for all you are,
  all you do,
  and all you enable.
Your works in plain view
  bring joy to my soul
  and inspiration to my mind.
Ever-living,
  ever-moving,
    ever-loving God:
  I seek to honour you in every way today.
Let the crude works of my hands
  be invaded by your glory,
  giving praise to you
  in their yet unformed state.
Let what I produce bear the imprint of the maker,
  bearing silent witness to the king of kings.
All I do is because of you!
You are the one who gives me breath
  and the only one worth living for.
Let your praises be on my lips
  and a song of worship in my heart;
  and may your glorious will be done here today.
Amen.

―――

2

DRAWING NEAR TO GOD

> 'But who am I, and who are my people, that we should
> be able to give as generously as this? Everything comes
> from you, and we have given you only what comes from
> your hand.'
> 1 CHRONICLES 29:14

When I was little, my parents would give me pocket money, which I would split into 'saving for later' and 'buying worthless tat'. Of course, I would not have called it that at the time. To a seven-year-old, it seemed like treasure to have my own anything – even if the rest of the family (and hindsight) could see it for what it was. The savings, though, had real value: I could use them to buy presents for others.

Effectively, I was only giving back to my parents what had already been theirs. One could argue that it was a poor return for their investment, given what I chose for them; but that would be missing the point. Their gift to me enabled me to try to show generosity and appreciation to them. It wasn't about the money.

David's words, quoted above, come towards the end of his life. His son, Solomon, has been anointed king and the great temple is no longer only being dreamed about but actually planned. He has pretty much emptied his coffers to help fund the project and encourages the leaders to do likewise. No arm-twisting was required. We read: 'The people rejoiced at the willing response of their leaders, for they had given *freely and wholeheartedly* to the Lord' (1 Chronicles 29:9; emphasis added).

I'll say it again: it wasn't about the money.

Sure, the temple could not have been constructed without funding, but giving to the Lord's work is rarely as simple as a matter of hard currency. 'Freely and wholeheartedly' is the takeaway phrase here. Giving their resources without looking sideways at what they might have been able to buy. Laying it at the altar without worrying how they would support their household.

David's question: 'Now, who is willing to consecrate themselves to the Lord today?' (1 Chronicles 29:5) is one we might do well to ask ourselves.

Am I offering myself freely and wholeheartedly to the Lord today?

Am I laying down all I have to be used in his service, knowing that everything comes from him?

Let this prayer, formerly attributed to St Ignatius, be our heart's cry today:

> *Lord, teach me to be generous,*
> *to serve you as you deserve,*
> *to give and not to count the cost,*
> *to fight and not to heed the wounds,*
> *to toil and not to seek for rest,*
> *to labour and not to look for any reward,*
> *save that of knowing that I do your holy will.*
> *Amen.*

Prayers of yielding

Therefore, I urge you, brothers and sisters, in view of God's mercy, to offer your bodies as a living sacrifice, holy and pleasing to God – this is your true and proper worship.

ROMANS 12:1

At the name of Jesus every knee should bow, in heaven and on earth and under the earth, and every tongue acknowledge that Jesus Christ is Lord, to the glory of God the Father.

PHILIPPIANS 2:10–11

God, I bow my knee before you.
You and you only are my Lord.
I have given up all rights to my life
*   and seek only to do your will.*
May my thinking align with yours;
*   may my attitudes be like Christ's.*
Teach me to walk your paths,
*   my hand firmly in yours.*
May I love the things you love
*   and reject the things you hate.*
I surrender my own thoughts, my own agenda.
Your will, not mine, be done,
*   through Jesus Christ,*
Amen.

———

God, you are Lord of the empty page,
  the blank canvas.
You took the darkness and emptiness
  of our pre-creation planet
  and brought light and life,
  order, potential and hope.
Would you do the same with me, for me, today?
Pierce my darkness –
  the shadowy areas I keep locked away –
  with light so bright, so dazzling,
  that there be no doubt
  your hand has touched me.

Pause to reflect

I am the empty page,
  the blank canvas,
  ready and yielded to you this day.
Do what you will;
  do what you must;
  for Jesus' sake,
  for your glory
  and for the benefit of all.
Amen.

———

God, all I am and have is yours.
I have already given you my heart –
    that day I came to my senses
    and handed you the reins of my life.
I have never had cause to regret that decision.
    In moments of doubt and confusion,
    clarity and elation,
    you have never ceased to be my Lord.

Pause to reflect

So, with open hands I come to you afresh today.
I lay down my own agenda,
    my own ideas about what may happen,
    and ask that you direct my steps.
Let my words reflect the truths
    you have planted in my mind.
Let my actions accord with your loving purpose.
May I do nothing that brings me shame
    or discredits your holy name.
You are Lord,
    my Lord,
        Lord of all.
Let everything I do today bring glory to you
    and satisfaction to my heart.
Amen.

––––

God, your word teaches that you are the potter,
  the hands-on God.
Your fingerprints are over every detail of my life.
I am the clay, surrendered to your skill.
As you shape me, squeeze me, form and remake me,
  let me not fight you, resist you or disagree with you.
Forgive me when I do –
  I am too used to being in charge,
  directing my own creations,
  missing the glorious metaphor before me.
So, before the day properly starts,
  I hand over to you my plans,
  my skills,
  my very being.
You are Lord.
You know best.
Let the peace springing from that truth
  sustain me today.
Have your way, my potter God.
Amen.

____

God, thank you for childhood,
*   not just as a caterpillar progression to the butterfly*
*   but for the uniqueness of being a child.*
You were careful to have Jesus invite them near.
You demonstrated acceptance of their state:
*   their silliness, messiness, muddled thinking;*
*   their lack of patience and self-control;*
*   their self-absorption.*
But – far more than that –
*   you embraced them for who they are,*
*   and in that I rejoice today.*
In making me creative,
*   you have kept part of my childhood*
*   in animated suspension.*
The joy of playing,
*   of handling raw material*
*   and wondering what will emerge.*
The losing sense of time,
*   caught up in the moment,*
*   all responsibility forgotten.*

→

The thrill of imagination
  bursting through reason
  and refusing to listen to common sense.
All these things are mine today
  as surely as when I was younger;
  and through them I come alive.
Thank you that I need not fear
  growing out of this phase,
  having to let go of childish ways
  for the sake of maturity.
Instead, I can embrace my inner child
  as surely as Jesus did,
  and welcome them into my day.
Let a child-like spirit,
  purified by your Holy Spirit,
  be present in my work-play today;
  and let what I create
  bring bubbles of joy
  and giggles of fun
  that put a smile on your face too.
Amen.

____

3

INSPIRATION

Poem

I walked today,
too rare a fine winter's day for aught else:
Sunny and chill,
its stillness creating a mirror
of the lake.
How I envy the artist!
There he was,
encased in down-filled layers,
a woollen beanie tight over his ears.
En plein air he stroked brush over canvas,
the trapped landscape unmistakeable.
Soulless were my phone's flat images.
And what of the writer and poet?
With mere black and white
they stimulate our senses
and fill our minds
with colour-fizzing potential.
They take us where we might never go,
lift our spirits up and away from human limits.

→

How blessed is the sculptor
and worker of matter,
inviting a touch,
a caress,
that could be our souls making the connection
and not our hands.
Each craft-worker, in unique ways,
raises their arms,
urging us likewise
to touch what remains just out of reach.
But on tiptoes we stand,
hoping,
striving,
longing
to recreate what God,
in his perfection,
has already wrought.

———

Prayers for inspiration and imagination

We pull down every proud obstacle that is raised against the knowledge of God; we take every thought captive and make it obey Christ.
2 CORINTHIANS 10:5 (GNT)

Now to him who is able to do immeasurably more than all we ask or imagine, according to his power that is at work within us, to him be glory in the church and in Christ Jesus throughout all generations, forever and ever! Amen.
EPHESIANS 3:20–21

'Forget the former things; do not dwell on the past. See, I am doing a new thing! Now it springs up; do you not perceive it? I am making a way in the wilderness and streams in the wasteland.'
ISAIAH 43:18–19

God, I come to you,
  in awe of your creative brilliance.
You made the entire human race in your image,
  building creativity
  into our thinking,
  into our very being.
Thank you.
Thank you for the gift of imagination,
  for the ability to create in my mind
  what does not yet exist.
I surrender my imagination to you today.
Let it not be a distraction
  that leads me away from you
  and all you have planned,
  but a tool you can use for your glory.
Expand my imagination, I pray.
Break off me all constraints
  imposed on me by others
  through their words and attitudes.

→

I am not delusional,
*   nor 'away with the fairies'!*
Hallelujah!
I rejoice and celebrate
*   that you created my mind*
*   full of imagined realities,*
*   a place of wonderment,*
*   of adventure!*
How grateful I am
*   that you gifted me with creativity*
*   to explore, share and express.*
Come, Holy Spirit,
*   stir my imagination today.*
Let all that I create
*   be uniquely inspired by you*
*   and bring you glory.*
Amen.

___

God, today I pray that you lift me up,
*   away from the humdrum,*
*   the ordinary.*
Let me refuse to take those well-trodden trails
*   that tempt me to lean*
*   on my own strength,*
*   my own, limited thinking.*
You are higher, greater,
*   deeper than I can imagine.*
What you reveal to me
*   blows my mind!*
I can be so blinkered,
*   so fixated on my own intentions*
*   that I forget your promise*
*   to do a new thing.*

→

Expand not only my imagination
  but my faith, Lord!
Lead me into uncharted places,
  beyond the safe,
    beyond the tried and tested.
I want to see this side of you, God:
  not only doing a new thing
  but a brand-new,
  never-before-seen thing.
Oh, that you would do this in and through me!
Do not delay, God.
Let me catch a glimpse
  of all you have been planning,
  and may I run after it
  with all my strength and energy.
Amen.

———

God, you have put the word 'fresh'
    on my mind today.
How timely that is!
I have been so tired lately,
    so wearied by life's mediocrity.
My soul is yearning for more,
    and I tune into its cry.
I think of early morning walks –
    am I the only one alive? –
    the grass still laden with dew,
    the air damp as I breathe it in.
In those moments,
    I sense all creation's expectations
    for the new day:
    a lesson about mine.
Refresh me, Lord.
Re-fresh me.

→

Shift my perspective,
  tipping my chin or cheek
  to face the right direction,
  to catch what you are pointing out.
Strip away my impatience to get going
  and compel me to linger.
Let the sense of the new,
  the unseen,
  the not-yet-experienced,
  lift me soul, mind and body.
Do such a creative,
  re-creative
  work in me
  that it spills into all that I make.
Let the wonder of creative potential
  be fulfilled in me,
  yes, even me.
Amen.

———

Prayers around colour

'I have set my rainbow in the clouds, and it will be the sign of the covenant between me and the earth.'
GENESIS 9:13

'So send me a master craftsman who can work with gold, silver, bronze, and iron, as well as with purple, scarlet, and blue cloth. He must be a skilled engraver who can work with the craftsmen of Judah and Jerusalem who were selected by my father, David.'
2 CHRONICLES 2:7 (NLT)

The wall was made of jasper, and the city of pure gold, as pure as glass. The foundations of the city walls were decorated with every kind of precious stone. The first foundation was jasper, the second sapphire, the third agate, the fourth emerald, the fifth onyx, the sixth ruby, the seventh chrysolite, the eighth beryl, the ninth topaz, the tenth turquoise, the eleventh jacinth, and the twelfth amethyst.
REVELATION 21:18–20

God, I want to thank you for colour:
* for when it is vivid and uplifting*
* or subtle and soothing.*
Thank you for its infinite variety:
* the myriads of shades,*
*   tones,*
*   hues.*
Thank you for the effect of colour
* deep within me as I work with it:*
* joy released,*
* sorrow expressed,*
* pain transformed.*
Thank you that you are not a dull God!
Through colour, you expose your heart
* for all you have created –*
* and that includes me!*
Today, let me be a living, colourful expression
* of your touch on my life.*
Amen.

———

God, I am aware today of the power of colour.
I'm mindful – carefully thoughtful –
  of how I will use colour today.
Will I play it safe?
Stick with the expected?
Will I shock,
  be misunderstood,
  even alienate?
Lord, let my provoking be under your control.
Let my instincts be under your Lordship.
Teach me, train me to choose colour well
  and to blend it skilfully.
Give me wisdom
  as I tune myself into your guiding,
  so that you can reach into people's hearts
  and your will be done through my choices.
The colours of heaven defy description.
I long to see a glimpse of heaven in this earthly realm
    today.
Amen.

———

God, what a gift of grace and mercy colour is!
The world was formless, chaotic
*   and shrouded in darkness*
*   until you spoke words*
*   that allowed a glimpse of heaven in:*
'Let there be light!'
*   and not just white light –*
*   the cosmic equivalent of flicking the switch*
*   to activate the bulb –*
*   but a rainbow riot!*
The beam refracting into hues
*   never before seen.*
How kind you are,
*   how thoughtful,*
*   that you did not permit a monochrome universe.*
How dull would be our days,
*   how narrow our understanding*
*   of who you are.*
You dwell in such indescribable glory
*   that no human words can approximate,*
*   no human works can emulate.*
All we can do is stop in wonder
*   and worship.*
The glory is yours, sublime God,
*   forever and ever.*
Amen.

———

For the writer

> God, I work in black letters on a screen;
>   in ink and graphite on a page:
>   nothing but stems, curls and cross-bars
>   and yet…
>   and yet within them –
>   miracle of miracles –
>   is life and light and colour!
> How is it possible?
> How can we 'see' a glorious landscape through mere
>   words?
> How can we understand thoughts and feelings,
>   motives and actions –
>   in all their technicolour complexity –
>   through these scribbled scratchings?
> It is all a mystery and a marvel!
> All I can do in response is thank you,
>   worship you
>   and ask that you continue
>   to breathe life, light and colour
>   through my paltry words.
> Amen.

―――

Poem

Take the dust of my design –
tiny particles they seem,
of no singular consequence or value.
I lay them out before you,
pondering together what we can make of them,
and how
and why.
A mystery it is, the creative process.
The nothing into something,
the not-yet into now.
Disparate components
unrelated, unconnected,
drawn together,
beautified,
dignified.
Perfection lies distant,
beyond mortal humanity,
yet tantalisingly,
exquisitely, near
in the immanence of your presence.
Take the dust of my design –
tiny particles though they seem.

———

4

PRAYERS AROUND GETTING STARTED

In the beginning God created the heavens and the earth. Now the earth was formless and empty, darkness was over the surface of the deep, and the Spirit of God was hovering over the waters.
GENESIS 1:1–2

Take delight in the Lord, and he will give you the desires of your heart.
PSALM 37:4

'Do not despise these small beginnings, for the Lord rejoices to see the work begin.'
ZECHARIAH 4:10 (NLT)

God, I acknowledge you as creator.
In the beginning, you spoke
  into chaos and darkness,
  emptiness and void,
  bringing forth life,
    substance,
    order.
I believe – I know –
  you can do the same today.
You see the tangle of my thinking,
  the areas of confusion and mess.
You see the fear and faltering,
  diffidence and hesitation.
Please speak fresh words of re-creation over me.
Without you I can do nothing.
Let there be light on the path that stretches before me.
Let there be life and reality
  instead of only the wistfulness of anticipation.
Take my ideas,
  my half-formed day-dreamings,
  and bring them into fullness of being.
I yield to you,
  creator,
  life-giver,
  true source of inspiration.
Amen.

———

God, I come in praise to you, in awe of you.
Who am I, compared with you?
I am nothing and nobody;
* yet you welcome me into your presence.*
You have chosen me to be yours,
* given me salvation*
* through the willing,*
* costly*
* sacrifice of Jesus.*
All that I am,
* everything I have,*
* is due to your grace-filled generosity.*

Pause in gratitude

And here I am before you:
* needing a fresh in-filling of the Holy Spirit,*
* so I can tune into your will and purposes today.*
The time allotted to me is precious.
The plans you have for my hours
* are greater than I can know.*
Help me be aware of your nudges today,
* your whispers into my heart,*
* guiding my thinking and my doing.*
Bless the end of this day
* with the satisfaction of knowing*
* we have travelled together,*
* working in tandem,*
* sharing the pleasure of creativity.*
Amen.

_____

God, today is the day.
I've dreamed for long enough,
  planned and re-planned,
  researched and revised.
It's time to commit to starting!
I'm excited, that is true,
  but I have to confess
  I am nervous.
It has felt safe so far.
Nothing has gone wrong yet;
  no one has polluted it with negative words;
  everything is to play for.
But all that is about to change.
What if I'm not as ready as I thought?
What if it comes out differently,
  or takes on a life of its own
  (that I can't control)?

→

Doubts are creeping in;
  my self-confidence is nose-diving.
I am tempted to put off the moment,
  give myself more time;
  but, instead, I'm choosing to look to you.
You are the one who gave me the ideas,
  set off those initial bursts of enthusiasm.
I have sensed your presence
  as I've explored what I can create,
  letting those tiny seeds take root
  in my heart and mind.
Be true to your word, Lord.
You rejoice to see the work start
  so I'm picking up the metaphorical spade,
  making the first cut of the soil!
Give me courage, Lord;
  give me strength.
And, at the end of this day,
  and the next,
    and the next,
  give me satisfaction in what I have created.
Amen.

———

5

ENCOURAGEMENT

Joseph, a Levite from Cyprus, whom the apostles called
Barnabas (which means 'son of encouragement'), sold
a field he owned and brought the money and put it at
the apostles' feet.
ACTS 4:36–37

Your love has given me great joy and encouragement,
because you, brother, have refreshed the hearts of the
Lord's people.
PHILEMON 1:7

Who doesn't love a 'Well done', a 'You've got this', or a 'I'm here
for you'? I hadn't quite appreciated the importance of those
little pep mottos until I began living on my own and there was
no one to cheer me on. I soon felt the lack of encouragement.
And let's be clear: that 'lack of encouragement' translated
into far more than the silence of absent words. I found myself
lethargic, uncertain, prone to give up quickly and even feeling low. My solution? I began saying out loud to myself what
I needed to hear: 'That looks great!'; 'I'm proud of you!'; 'You
were brave today!'

Even as I was writing this reflection, I felt prompted to pop a
message on WhatsApp to my colleagues: 'How is everyone
doing today?' The responses came through quickly. Most were
having a busy old time and seemed to appreciate the sense
of team-work. One telling comment was this: 'Thanks for
creating a safe space where we can be real.' And that's the
thing about encouragement: it feeds both the giver and the
receiver. Both feel a measure of joy at being noticed and mat-
tering to someone.

Many of us will have been schooled within a climate of criticism rather than encouragement, the teachers believing that telling us we were inadequate would somehow inspire us to greater things. For a few, it did provoke them into 'proving *them* wrong' and they shrugged off their low expectations as they broke into a run. For too many, though, the burden of being seen as an under-achiever was one they ended up shouldering for the rest of their days.

It is my sincere and earnest hope that when I die, I shall hear God saying to me, 'Well done, good and faithful servant' (Matthew 25:23). It is an equal hope that I will sense that phrase over me every day of my life; that his encouragement would be a constant source of strength as I serve him.

> *When others neglect to say a word – you cheer me on.*
> *When their thoughtlessness leaves me cold – you cheer*
> *   me on.*
> *When my work is misunderstood, undermined – you cheer*
> *   me on.*
> *When I lose my way, no help to find – you cheer me on.*

Prayers for encouragement

Why do you complain, Jacob? Why do you say, Israel, 'My way is hidden from the Lord; my cause is disregarded by my God'? Do you not know? Have you not heard? The Lord is the everlasting God, the Creator of the ends of the earth.

ISAIAH 40:27–28

Know that the Lord has set apart his faithful servant for himself; the Lord hears when I call to him.

PSALM 4:3

God, speaker of the truer word,
  must I wait until glory to hear,
  'Well done, good and faithful servant'?
Let me sense you saying it over me today
  because it would help me carry on.
So many crucial tasks and processes seem thankless,
  unnoticed.
Do you see me, God?
Do you notice the efforts I put in
  behind the scenes?

Pause to reflect

Thank you for the encouragement to my soul
  that your word brings.
Of course you see me!
Lover of Hagar,
  defender of Rahab,
  champion of every lost and abandoned one;
  you have surely not overlooked me.
Silent or speaking,
  let me know your 'well done',
  for it is enough.
Amen.

_____

Lord, I'm feeling stuck.
I'm only part way in –
  barely past the entry sign –
  but already my bravado is slipping.
However did I think I could do this solo?
Over-confident,
  under-equipped;
  that's too familiar a story.
Thank you for always being there when I call
  (and, of course, even there when I don't).
I've prayed so many times over this
  but I need you in human form today.
I need someone else's eyes,
  someone's opinion.
Truthfully, I long for a hug,
  a pat on the shoulder –
  anything to break the isolation
  and tell me all is well.
Could I be on someone's mind today,
  someone who would message me
  some words of encouragement?
If not, then please nudge me
  to reach out to the right one;
  let them be free to take my call.
Let them have time to listen.
Please, Lord?
Amen.

———

God, I pray that today
  you would lead and guide me
  to be an encourager
  not through words alone
  but by action.
Show me practical ways
  I can support the endeavours
  of my fellow creatives.
Help me, though, to remain sensitive
  and treat them with dignity –
  not implying that I know better.
How we all need you, Lord!
Let me be open to your prompting,
  whatever it may be.
Help me not hold back
  from buying what they have created,
  not thinking of the price
  but only of its value.

→

You have given me all I need for life,
  all without cost or merit,
  so let me extend that same grace to others.
Show me if I can be a door-opener,
  as others have been for me;
  making connections that might propel them
  higher and further.
I long to lift their spirits today,
  to honour their efforts
  and champion their craft.
I trust you to bless them, Lord,
  however you choose,
  because your ways are always best.
In the meantime, I pray
  your richest blessings on them
  and all they create today.
Let us all be rejoicing
  when the evening comes.
Amen.

———

6

MID-PROJECT CHALLENGES,
A.K.A. THE MESSY MIDDLE

Creatives know all about the pull of imagination. Those count-less times a day when we see something, or hear something, or think about anything at all and *boom!* there it is. Before we know it, our hearts are pounding out an adrenalin-fuelled thump, our minds are whirling, and we're reaching for some-thing to write it down on before we forget. (I beg, urge and plead with you to carry a notebook with you at all times – particularly inconvenient times, which is when most inspiration strikes!)

Starting a new project is FUN. Getting the workspace set up, laying out our materials and ideas. At this stage, all we are focused on are the possibilities. Forget all we've ever done before, all that matters is this new one, the one we've been working up to all our lives! It could be the turning point! The sky is the limit! And, of course – since we are being delusional, let's add to the nonsense – we will knock it out in no time!

I thank God for these early stages, I truly do. Without a detach-ment from reality, we would never want to get started. (If some-one laid out the costs – the finances, the aches and pains, the lack of human company, the sheer effort in every area – we would run a mile and stick to the day job.) Then, once enthu-siasm has hitched its wagon on to this dream-like state, we're off, and the new project is underway.

We might only be a tiny way in before reality starts to bite. The early wins quickly fade and the going gets tougher. If you've ever been on a ramble and got caught up in marshy ground, you'll know that feeling of being too far in to turn back and not far enough on to be soon safely home in the warm. The dilemma is real. Do you press on, risking wet feet and worse, or turn back, still with wet feet and – more to the point – crushing disappointment as your companion?

This marshy analogy is a fitting one for what I refer to as 'the messy middle'. For some of us, it involves the literal mess of art materials and the chaos of a workspace with an engaged sign on the door. For me, because the bulk of my creativity is expressed through writing, the mess is in my head (with inevitable spreadage on to the desk). Not only does this tend to result in scrambled thoughts and unclear plotting, but it can also contribute to poor sleep quality and general agitation.

Perhaps part of our difficulty is that our expectations are skewed, no matter how many times we find ourselves here. We can think that 'this time' we'll be more organised, more proactive, that we will have learned all the lessons from before. But, just as you wouldn't go out in the Lake District without wet weather gear, so we need to accept – unquestioningly – that the middle is *always* messy. It comes with the territory. There's no avoiding it.

What, then, can we do?

1 Don't panic. This is normal. What doesn't look a mess when it is part-formed?
2 Remind yourself of the plan. Tick off the steps you have already made and tackle the next one, nice and calmly.
3 Refuse all judgement, especially yours! (Your perspective is as skewed as your expectation, remember.)
4 Pray. For this – for all eventualities and for all time – we have Jesus.
5 Worship. He is still worthy of our devotion, and lifting our heads to look at him will help recalibrate our mind and our heart.
6 Trust: in God who called you to it, and in yourself. He is utterly able and he has resourced you to be capable.
7 Plan the celebration of the finish, even now. Keep your eyes on that goal!

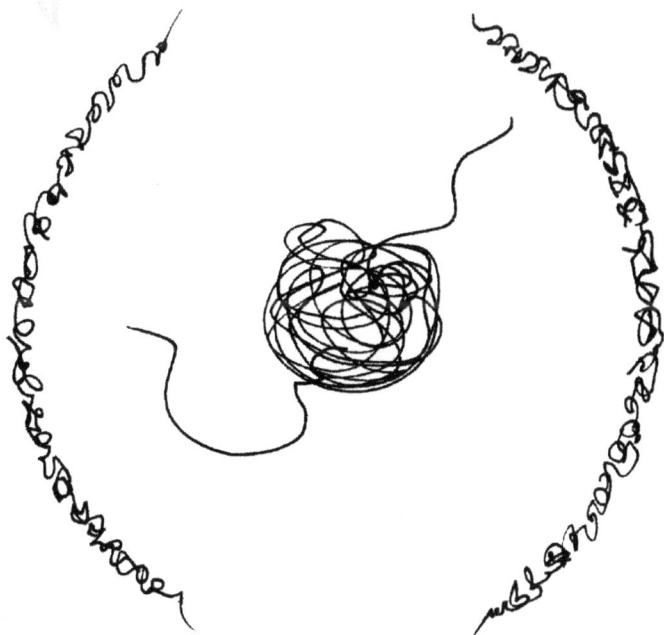

Prayers for the messy middle

My frame was not hidden from you when I was made in the secret place, when I was woven together in the depths of the earth. Your eyes saw my unformed body.
PSALM 139:15–16

So do not throw away your confidence; it will be richly rewarded. You need to persevere so that when you have done the will of God, you will receive what he has promised.
HEBREWS 10:35–36

I am the Alpha and the Omega, the First and the Last, the Beginning and the End.
REVELATION 22:13

God, I acknowledge the truth:
* you are the Alpha and the Omega,*
* the Beginning and the End.*
Without you, there is no project,
* no purpose,*
* no point.*
Thank you for helping me get started:
* for dealing with my fears,*
* for inspiring me with ideas,*
* for prompting my spirit.*
But I'm in the 'messy middle', Lord.
I've started;
* the end will be a long time coming.*
Sometimes, I'm in a tunnel
* with no light at the end;*
* the familiar tracks of past projects*
* lying behind me.*
Other times, I'm up to my elbows in raw material,
* but no discernible shape emerging.*
It's hard.
Plain hard.
Dare I push on,
* squash my emotions down,*
* and just get on with it?*
Can I?

→

How I long to turn a corner,
  feel the spring returning to my feet,
  in hope of accelerating towards the finish,
  where you are waiting to greet me.
But, oh Lord,
  that feels a light year away.
I'm getting so discouraged by the slog.
Tell me:
  are you a God of the middle too?
I want to trust that you are.
Help me keep believing
  you will bring to completion what you have begun.
(Surely that means you're present in the process?)
Your word convinces me
  that you will never leave me nor forsake me
  but please let me be aware of your presence today.
Give me eyes to see what isn't yet formed.
Let joy spring up,
  born of hope.
You're a good God and I love you.
All glory to you –
  even in this.
Amen.

―――

God, I regret starting this.
Forgive my impetuousness,
  my impatience
    again.
I have dived in,
  not wearing goggles
  but blinkers;
  blind to reality.
Yet I am too far in to turn around.
If I gave up now,
  I would be letting myself down
  and others too.
Including you, God,
  I suspect.

Pause to reflect

→

Thank you for reminding me:
  I have a choice.
I can either close the door on it all
  and walk away
  or I can pray a new prayer:
  'God, grow me.'
Teach me something of yourself
  in this uncomfortable place.
Take away agitation;
  give me your peace and serenity.
Remind me who is in charge,
  that there is a God and it is not me!
Then take my hand –
  I offer it freely –
  and lead me through,
  each step placed for your glory.
Amen.

___

God, I want to pray about how long this is taking;
  the sheer number of hours I'm spending on this.
Procrastination and time-wasting
  have turned this hoped-for sprint
  into a marathon.
Even now,
  when I am trying to focus on you,
  my mind is wandering.
Forgive me, Lord.
Have I got what it takes?
Is everything I start doomed never to be completed?
I am stuck.
I don't like it.
Help me through this phase, please.
Increase not just my resilience but my tenacity.
Keep me at my post until I have seen it through.
It will be such a miracle
  when I reach the other side
  that all will know it was you!
Help me now;
  help me always.
Amen.

God, I turn to you,
  my counsellor, helper and encourager.
Come and settle my heart and mind
  as I pour out my worries to you.
I feel guilty, Lord.
Guilty that others are affected by me doing what I love.
I exist in an otherworldly bubble of creating,
  neglecting my family,
  ignoring my friends.
How often have I promised:
  'Yes, soon – when this piece is finished'?
Only for that moment to be delayed.
Again.

Pause to reflect

→

And I'm mindful of those who bear the cost;
 foot the bills;
 offer kindness and generosity,
 so precious
 and so embarrassingly necessary.
I hear the wisdom of getting a 'proper job'
 but my creativity compels me,
 drives me;
 I come alive;
 my heart is satisfied.
Without it, I would wither away and die,
 but…
I don't want to create victims of my loved ones.
Give me wisdom, Lord.
Bring peace to my heart;
 funds into my account.
Give patience and understanding to those I love.
Thank you, God.
Amen.

———

Prayers for creative blockage

'Truly I tell you, if anyone says to this mountain, "Go, throw yourself into the sea," and does not doubt in their heart but believes that what they say will happen, it will be done for them.'

MARK 11:23

'Other seed fell among thorns, which grew up with it and choked the plants... The seed that fell among thorns stands for those who hear, but as they go on their way they are choked by life's worries, riches and pleasures, and they do not mature.'

LUKE 8:7, 14

'Ask and it will be given to you; seek and you will find; knock and the door will be opened to you. For everyone who asks receives; the one who seeks finds; and to the one who knocks, the door will be opened.'

MATTHEW 7:7–8

God, thank you for prompting me to pray,
  to turn away from this nothingness
  and seek you,
  the God who never fails.
As for me,
  I've drawn a blank.
I've lowered my bucket into the well
  and it's come up empty –
  though it is worse than that.
I could almost live with the dead space
  if it weren't full of disappointment,
    frustration,
      panic.
Can I do it again?
Was my last creation really that:
  the last?
Am I done?

Pause to take deep breaths

→

God, into my head,
  my full-of-anxiety,
  devoid-of-ideas head,
  comes a promise:
  that if I seek you –
    no, more than that –
  if I knock, pounding the doors of heaven,
  you will answer;
    and when you do,
  I will ask, and you will listen,
  and care
  and act like it matters to you too.
Then you will bend down,
  look me in the eye –
  I feel better even thinking about it –
  and give me what I'm asking for,
  because you are a good God.
Oh, Lord, thank you!
Thank you for hope rising,
  for peace descending,
  and, please, please,
  for ideas coming.
Amen.

_____

God, please come when I call!
I've been sitting here,
  lost in thoughts that by no stretch
  can be called creative.
I've walked.
I've journalled.
I've read that tips book,
  listened to that podcast
  yet again.
If I could convert the effort
  of excuses and prevarication
  into something akin to momentum,
  that would be not just
  prayers answered,
  a dream come true,
  but a miracle for sure.
Is it time, Lord?
Time to stand on your word,
  to tell that Mount Creative Block
  to take a running jump into the sea?
I've been praying that you'll do it –
  you're so much stronger than me.
But I read again and see that it says,
  'If anyone says to this mountain…'*
Can I, weakened and outfaced by this obstacle,
  can I be an anyone
  and tell it just to go?

Pause to let faith rise.

*Mark 11:23

→

I trust you, God.
Your word does not tease or disappoint.
So, in the name of Jesus,
the rock on which I stand,
I command this mere pebble,
that dares to challenge what you've birthed in me,
to go!
Let it be so, Lord!
Amen and amen.

_____

God, there is so much of life
I cannot do alone.
The blessing of your constant presence
reminds me how much
I need you.
Thank you for hearing the prayers I'm offering
amid the tangle of my life
right now.
My head is that field where good seed
is being choked
by all that I carry.
Preoccupied, in its truest sense,
by the mental equivalent of
thistles and brambles.

Pause to reflect

→

Lord, I want to be fertile soil.
I want your touch on my life
  to till me,
  rake out the rubbish,
  nourish me,
  body, mind, soul and spirit.
Maybe, then, the ideas will flow?
The joy of working in harness with you
  will turn the drought into a trickle,
  into a stream,
  then a flood!
Meantime, keep working on and in me,
  for me and through me.
Let this dry spell bear its own unique fruit.
I choose to trust you, God.
I choose to worship you.
I offer my thanks for all you will do.
Amen.

———

Prayers for confusion and anxiety

You will keep in perfect peace all who trust in you, all whose thoughts are fixed on you!
ISAIAH 26:3 (NLT)

The Lord says, 'I will rescue those who love me. I will protect those who trust in my name.'
PSALM 91:14 (NLT)

God, my mind is whirling.
How hard it is today to stop long enough to pray
  when my thoughts are making me restless.
Peace is absent.
Joy is forgotten.
Into the eddy comes the temptation
  to harness this surging energy to my workload;
  forget my 'quiet time';
  just get on.
Surely later, reasons a voice not my own,
  I'll be more settled,
  better able to concentrate.
Lord, have mercy.
Pent-up mental energy offers
  only pseudo-strength.
I need more than raw, brute momentum:
  let me savour the all-embracing, all-sufficient power,
  coming from the very throne room of heaven.

Pause to reflect

→

I choose to let go of all anxiety,
  and all its attendant agitation.
I choose to pause;
  to look to you;
  to take a breath,
    and another,
      and another.
I call to mind the promises of scripture:
  though it feels like the biggest battle,
  I will resolutely fix my thoughts on you.
As I surrender to your truth,
  let peace overwhelm me;
  let it overflow into all I seek to achieve today.
Hand in hand, with you, dear God,
  my mind renewed,
  let us go into the day together.
Amen.

———

God, I'm feeling afraid.
Having to create something,
   to 'come up with the goods',
   can feel overwhelming,
   the responsibility exhausting.
Sometimes, I'm riding the waves,
   exhilarated, buoyed along.
All too soon, those same waves can threaten to
     push me under,
   their power working against me.
I know the first step is to be honest,
   hard though it is.
So, I'm not going to dress this up,
   making it look different.
I'm not going to bottle this up inside
   but speak it out loud,
   risky though it may be.

→

I'm scared.
I'm nervous.
But you love me;
*   you never leave me nor forsake me –*
*   no matter how I'm feeling.*
I call to mind your promises
*   and plant my feet firmly on their truth.*
I do love you, Lord;
*   I do trust you,*
*   even when I don't feel brave.*
Rescue me, I pray, from all my fears and worries.
Restore my confidence.
Renew my peace.
Thank you for all you are about to do.
Amen.

_____

God, I want to thank you today
for the sensitivity you have woven through me.
I don't have a thick skin
nor a hard heart.
I'm fragile –
sometimes hopelessly so –
but perish the alternative!
In feeling and thinking things that others don't,
I can communicate your ways
that enrich life,
nourish souls.
Oh, but sometimes,
sometimes,
I'm battered and bruised,
left reeling from pressures
others know nothing about.
I can't let things slide,
shrug it all off.
So, let me do today
what I must do:
pray.

Pause to reflect

→

I pray that as I pour these anxieties into the work of my
     hands,
   you would weave gold into the cracks.
Let me not hide my inner brokenness
   but instead let you transform it
   into outward beauty.
All those who behold what I have made,
   who hold it in their hands,
   or mull it in their minds –
   let them be shaken in their hearts
   by what you can do.
Amen.

_____

God, I'm confused.
Yesterday my mind was clear,
  my intentions focused.
  I felt happy with what I'd created,
  the next steps certain.
I was so sure you wanted me to do this.
Today, though, something has changed.
My head feels woolly,
  my heart heavy.
Soul, why are you downcast within me?
What does all this mean?
Do I stop, take stock?
Is it you, Lord, staying my hand,
  holding me back?
Or is this the enemy,
  trying to thwart my (your) plans?
I never quite know.
Am I wasting my time?
Did I misunderstand your commission?
Did you even speak in the first place?
None of my answers bring clarity or peace;
  God, I need you!
Shine your light into the fog.
Take the fragments of my thinking
  and rework them.
I surrender my agenda.

Pause to reflect

→

Let peace come
  in yielding myself to you afresh.
I lay everything at your feet,
  trusting you will show me what to pick up again,
  and when.
Your will be done, Lord.
Amen.

―――

7

THE LONELINESS OF THE
LONG-DISTANCE CREATIVE

Near to where I live is a community art gallery. It's a great place to mosey round whenever I'm in the area, which is not as often as I would like. Perhaps it's as well: the temptation to come away with yet another hand-crafted piece is hard to resist. The back of the former grocery store, which once housed the freezers, is now home to a number of paint-splattered tables and chairs and, usually, paint-splattered people. The last time I was there, the entire space was filled with riotous laughter. An afternoon workshop (both the medium and subject matter irrelevant, you understand) was obviously doing what creativity does best: lifting the spirits, filling the soul and connecting the attendees with like-minded (and -hearted) folk.

This is not the norm, however. In art studios, workshops, sheds, spare bedrooms, kitchens and wherever there is a free corner, creatives of all types beaver away at their work-in-progress on their own.

Free from distractions and other people's noise pollution, the solitary hours can be stimulating and fulfilling. It's perhaps as well that I like to write alone, as I am so caught up with what is in my head that I would be no company for anyone with me.

There is a fine line, though, between aloneness and loneliness, solitude and isolation. Just how fine that line is can come as a surprise sometimes. One minute, we're preoccupied with the task, content in our own bubble; the next, we find ourselves craving a 'well done', an approving nod – anything from anyone, in fact. A day that starts with contentment and satisfaction can unravel into a low mood or worse at the least provocation.

As Christians, we utterly believe God's promise to never leave or forsake us. We also know we can sense him through the Holy Spirit's presence. Truly, we can say that we are never alone. But, but… there is a reason we have been created as we are. We simply don't thrive in quite the same way when we have no company. While aloneness for a time can be energising in its own way, prolonged isolation – such as a creative-at-work might experience on a frequent basis – is not good for the soul. That presence of God, which fills us up on so many occasions, has to be clothed in skin sometimes to hit the spot.

Here are a few tips I recommend:

- Seek out company – or move away from what you are doing – *before* a problem starts.
- Be honest: learn how to recognise the telltale signs that the fine line has been crossed.
- Join a collective or association and go to their get-togethers.
- Be creative with a friend or colleague.

And, finally, 'Above all else, guard your heart, for everything you do flows from it' (Proverbs 4:23).

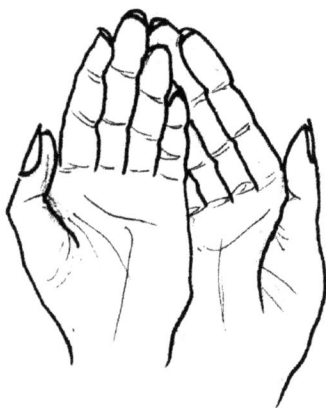

Prayers around aloneness

And you are to rejoice before the Lord your God in everything you put your hand to.
DEUTERONOMY 12:18

You, God, are my God, earnestly I seek you; I thirst for you, my whole being longs for you, in a dry and parched land where there is no water.
PSALM 63:1

'Call to me and I will answer you.'
JEREMIAH 33:3

God, here I am again,
  in my creative space.
Thank you for the blessing of it!
The potential of it!
It is the place I can come
  to indulge in what I love doing the most.
What a gift!
You have answered so many of my prayers and I'm
    grateful.
Thank you for peace as I work alone,
  uninterrupted.
Thank you that there is no one to distract me;
  I'm focused.
Thank you.

Pause to reflect

Oh, how I thank you that I am never truly alone!
Your presence is a constant,
  here and everywhere.
When I need help, you are here.
When I speak into the air, you hear it.
When I'm stuck, you point out the next step.
Glorious God, what a team we make!
It might look as if I am here on my own,
  but I am surrounded by the very hosts of heaven!
Hallelujah!
Amen!

____

God, the balance has tipped:
*   'alone' has become 'lonely'.*
Isolation is starting to bite.
I craved peace; now I long for discussion.
I valued independence; now I long for collaboration.
I prayed for single-minded focus; but I need fresh
*   perspective.*
I need someone else here.
I yearned for no interruptions; but I long to be made a cup
*   of tea!*
I wanted no distractions; but I'm trapped in my own head.
I thought I was resilient; but I want some encouragement.
I need someone else here.
Would you send someone, Lord,
*   and keep me steady until they arrive – if they do?*
You are enough and plenty,
*   in good times and tough.*
I choose to turn away my loneliness
*   at the door,*
*   as I welcome you in as my companion.*
Amen.

———

God, I thought I would always love being here, doing this;
  but I have to confess, Lord,
  I do not always appreciate being on my own.
I need to say it out loud:
  sometimes I just don't like it.
I hear that sounds ungrateful;
  I am sorry.
Please break the sense of isolation.
Give me wisdom: do I stay at my post
  or seek out company?
Please send your Holy Spirit;
  fill this space with your presence
  and satisfy the longings of my soul.
In Jesus' name,
Amen.

———

God, I need you.
That is always true,
  but today, my heart is saying it louder.
I need you.
I need you because there is no one else here,
  and no one I can call on.
You have promised to answer me when I call to you,
  so, here it is:
  come, Lord, please.
Amen.

———

8

KEEPING OURSELVES AND
OUR MOTIVES PURE

Character focus
Demetrius, the silver-idol maker

About that time there arose a great disturbance about the Way. A silversmith named Demetrius, who made silver shrines of Artemis, brought in a lot of business for the craftsmen there… '[Paul] says that gods made by human hands are no gods at all. There is danger not only that our trade will lose its good name, but also that the temple of the great goddess Artemis will be discredited…'
ACTS 19:23–24, 26–27

[Aaron] took what they handed him and made it into an idol cast in the shape of a calf, fashioning it with a tool. Then they said, 'These are your gods, Israel, who brought you up out of Egypt.'
EXODUS 32:4

I came across this statement in one of those jokey kind of gift books: 'Face it. It could be that the purpose of your life is only to serve as a warning to others.' I laughed hard at the time – I wonder if anyone sprang to mind for you, as they did for me?

So often we look to the Bible for inspiration, seeking out examples of great women and men of faith through whom we can learn our own life lessons. But, of course, it's not only the success stories that teach us. There are plenty of instances, too, where the people serve as warnings that we must heed.

Meet Demetrius. He was a skilled silversmith based in Ephesus, no doubt working in a collective, specialising in making shrines – focal points of worship – of the Greek goddess of hunting. I don't doubt they were exquisite. These were no tacky, commercial trinkets. They would have commanded a high price and, no doubt, a high level of devotion from Artemis' worshippers. Paul had stood up to idolatry before, but this time his opposition was levelled at a whole industry.

You see, as Christian creatives we must never lose sight of the fact that, whatever our craft, what we produce should bring glory to God. If it detracts from him or, worse still, consciously points to another 'god', then we are on very dodgy ground indeed. We cannot attribute our skills and expertise to God while at the same time dishonouring him.

The Bible mentions silver many times, in both material and spiritual contexts. Perhaps because of the way that silver is produced – the ultra-heating that burns away the dross – it is a symbol for the way God calls us to purify our hearts. I suggest that this applies not only to sin but to our heart attitudes too.

And what of Aaron? The story of the golden calf might well be a familiar one. Moses had gone up the mountain to receive the ten commandments, and he stayed away a long time, long enough for the people to get restless. Wanting to appease them, Aaron called for their jewellery and melted it down, fashioning it into a false god and encouraging their worship of it.

Do you see the danger for us here? Aaron was a priest, set apart for holy living, understanding something of who this God Yahweh was. Yet even he could be led astray when under pressure. His life was dedicated to God, but his actions denied it.

Yes, indeed, Demetrius and Aaron serve as warnings.

Let us be those in whom God has done a refining work: pure in heart, pure in output – for his glory.

Prayers for purity

All a person's ways seem pure to them, but motives are weighed by the Lord.
PROVERBS 16:2

When you ask, you do not receive, because you ask with wrong motives, that you may spend what you get on your pleasures.
JAMES 4:3

God, I worship you,
  echoing the cry of the seraphim:
  'Holy, holy, holy!'
Nothing and no one compare with you,
  the only one worthy to be called awesome.
I cannot fathom your absolute purity,
  the untarnishable nature of your goodness.
I can only bow in recognition of my own sinfulness
  and be grateful that, through Jesus, I am welcome.
In you is no double standard,
  no pretence,
  no pride.
My heart's cry is that I be more like you!
I'm so aware of the base instinct that drives me
  to seek my own glory and not yours.
Forgive me, Lord, when I let the gifts you have given
  eclipse the giver.
Remind me, hour by hour,
  of your pre-eminence.
Deal with my sin,
  pour out your grace,
  make me pure, I pray.
Amen.

———

God, I was flattered today.
Those comments on what I had done
   encouraged me so much;
   but, though I thanked you as the source of it all,
   I kept some of the glory for myself.
I'm sorry.
I find it so hard to keep my heart pure
   and my motivation centred on you.
I am so very grateful for all you do in and through me
   and acknowledge that I'm useless without you,
   and yet…
I feel a shift in me sometimes,
   a little voice that tempts me to take the credit.
Give me a greater vision of you, Lord!
Let me be so confronted by your majesty
   that I forever know my place:
   redeemed by the blood of Jesus
   and saved through no work of my own.
Amen.

———

God, you have my devotion.
When you told me you loved me,
   I believed you,
   and my life was forever changed.
Every day, my prayer is that I stay
   close to your heart,
   tuned into your will,
   humbled in your presence.
I lay down my own motivation
   and ask that you fill me again
   with your Holy Spirit.

Pause to reflect

Come as a fire,
   burning away the dross and all impurity.
Come as the wind,
   blowing away my fickleness and making me steadfast.
Come as the reminder of truth,
   recentring my soul upon your word.
Let all I do today bring honour and glory
   to your name and yours alone.
Amen.

_____

God, I could have made the golden calf.
I want to read that story and think poorly of Aaron,
    pompously dismissing his actions
    as those of a fickle heart.
Surely I would know better?
Not give into temptation?
Yet my heart whispers the truth:
    it could have been me.
I could have been the one
    who despaired of delay,
    considered you absent,
    then created a god of my own.
Haven't I replaced you before,
    establishing myself as arbiter,
        decision-maker,
            boss?
Haven't I become impatient,
    convinced I know better,
    conjuring solutions?
Forgive me, God,
    for calling you 'Lord'
    then acting as if you are not.
Pride is such a besetting sin –
    and denial of it only adds to its shame.
Let my creativity never stand in opposition to you
    but ever humble itself before you.
All honour and glory to you
    and thanksgiving that there is a God
        and it's not me.
Amen.

_____

9

REST

I am writing this on the sabbath. There is a sweet irony there: am I breaking my day of rest by working? Perhaps. Yet I am not at my desk but in my egg-chair, feeling the first half-decent sunshine on my wintry-pallid limbs and listening to birdsong. It's not my laptop open but a notebook, my handwriting creaking with unfamiliar use.

I am writing this reflection in rest, in an attitude of relaxation.

Working from rest.

This is what God intended all along. Not tired from six days of creating, but satisfied, fulfilled, God-rested. For Adam and Eve, it was their first full day in the garden of Eden, a place brimming and literally buzzing with life and possibility.

'What's the plan, God?' they say together, itching to get started.

God smiles, his heart touched by the joyful enthusiasm of these never-been-children humans. 'Rest,' he says.

'What's that?' they ask, looking around. 'Where do we find it?'

God chuckles and touches them lightly on shoulders that have never yet borne burdens. 'It's inside you. Let me show you how.'

It is a lesson we have refused to learn.

As creatives (never mind mere humans), we are used to the pull of the fresh idea, the kind of madness that consumes us as we work-play. Forgetting the mundanity of physical needs, we carry on without food or drink or comfort breaks. We hunch over until our bodies are locked into position. We fail to notice twilight creeping in beyond the window.

'Stop!' cry our loved ones/timetables/poor bodies. 'Rest!'

'What's that?' we ask.

The answer is the same as on that day seven of creation, though sometimes I think I hear not a chuckle but sorrow in the voice of the creator as he replies: 'It's inside you. Buried deep, buried for too long, but it's there. Let me show you how to find it. Then we'll practise together.'

This is what my soul craves – and yours, too, if you tune into it: not just the chance to stop but to intentionally disconnect from the strident busyness and reconnect with God.

Drop thy still dews of quietness,
till all our strivings cease;
take from our souls the strain and stress,
and let our ordered lives confess
the beauty of thy peace.
John Greenleaf Whittier (1807–92)

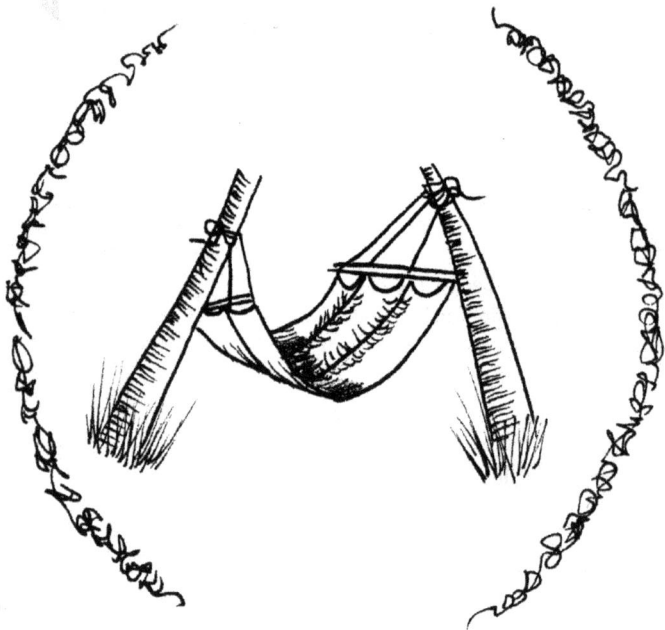

Prayers for rest

For in six days the Lord made the heavens and the earth,
the sea, and all that is in them, but he rested on the
seventh day. Therefore the Lord blessed the Sabbath
day and made it holy.
EXODUS 20:11

The Lord replied, 'My Presence will go with you, and
I will give you rest.'
EXODUS 33:14

Take my yoke upon you and learn from me, for I am
gentle and humble in heart, and you will find rest for
your souls.
MATTHEW 11:29

God, thank you for ordaining sabbath,
 a day when I can lay down my tools,
 let my hands and mind stop their striving,
 and simply be.
I'm tempted to carry on,
 as ever,
 to press on despite my tiredness,
 but I'm choosing to tune into your wisdom.
You know I tell myself I'm not really working
 since I love what I do,
 but you draw me out of excuses and into rest.

Pause to reflect

Laying down my tasks to embrace rest
 is like tithing my time
 as joyfully as I tithe my money.
I trust you, God, to do more with the fewer hours
 than burning the candle at both ends has ever done.
Do something, Lord, behind the scenes.
Refuel my energy,
 refill my mind,
 renew my zeal
 and refresh my concentration.
Let me enter tomorrow different from how I left yesterday.
But enough talk about tomorrow.
For now, I am stopping,
 drinking deeply from you
 and enjoying sabbath rest.
Amen.

———

God, thank you for the satisfaction
that follows times of exertion.
There is an odd joy in the exhaustion,
knowing I have become tired
doing such good, good things.
I close my eyes,
slow my breathing,
and consider you.

Pause to reflect

How your rest eases my muscles,
soothes my mind
and saturates my soul!
There is no place on earth
to feel peace so completely
than in your presence.
I need not revisit the events of my day
since you have seen every moment;
and not just seen
but understood.
As I surrender to your love,
you relieve me of every burden,
lift off every stress.
Let me stay here, sensing your nearness,
long enough for you to complete this work
of refreshing and restoration.
Prince of peace,
I worship you.
Amen.

———

God, I hear you call me into rest
  but I barely dare stop.
There never feels a good time to leave my work.
What if I forget the next stages?
What if I can't pick up the thread?
Surely it would render useless what I've done.
My mind tells me to keep going,
  but you speak a better word:
  'Come away with me, my love.'

Pause to reflect

It is only as I accept your hand,
  leading me into green pastures,
    that I realise the extent of my tiredness.
This is what I'm afraid of:
  that I will never get myself going again.
But then, I hear my words
  and see my error:
  it is not up to me.
I am not a machine,
  not invincible.
I am human,
  with frailty and weakness inbuilt
  so that – hallelujah –
  I always need a Saviour,
    a rescuer,
    a healer.
Amen.

____

God of order,
  Lord of time and space,
  invade the chaos of my inner world
  with your countercultural wisdom.
Turn upside-down my timetable
  born of drivenness;
  my routines
  inspired by stress;
  and my instincts
  rooted in long-learned thinking.
Your call to 'Rest, child, rest!'
  travels to my dull ears
  as if through fog –
  the words themselves clear
  but their meaning distorted.
And like a stubborn toddler
  I refuse the invitation,
  too wound up to even slow down,
  convinced I know better.
Forgive me, Lord,
  for taking such pride in my energy
  that I consider myself
  invincible,
  resisting your kind protection
  against crash and burn-out.
Teach me, Lord, what rest is,
  how good it could be.
I hear your call.
I heed your call.
I'm coming into your open arms.
Amen.

_____

God, your word tells me
  that in repentance and rest
  is my salvation;
    in quietness and trust
    is my strength.*
I confess that I have too often
  chosen to do differently.
I have seen pressing on as my strength,
  applauding my own resilience,
  ignoring your teaching,
  refusing your wisdom.

Pause to reflect

Teach me how to rest, Lord!
Show me your ways!
I confess to running on empty
  too much of the time.
I repent of hiding my weakness
  behind my smiles.

→

In your presence
  I choose to remove the mask,
  let go of the 'I'm fine'
    and sink to my knees.
I open up my heart
  for a refilling:
    of your Holy Spirit,
    of your precious anointing,
    of divinely sourced energy.
Pour rivers of peace over me,
  saturating me through and through.
Thank you, Lord.
Thank you for overruling my stubbornness,
  forgiving my obstinance
  and blessing me with rest.
Amen.

*See Isaiah 30:15

———

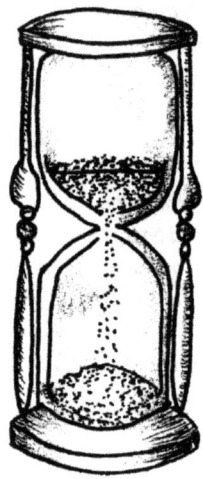

Time

Hour by hour I place my days
in your hand.
PSALM 31:15 (MSG)

The faithful love of the Lord never ends! His mercies
never cease.
    Great is his faithfulness; his mercies begin afresh
each morning.
LAMENTATIONS 3:22–23 (NLT)

If every one of the 86,400 seconds in every 24-hour period were pennies, I would consider myself rich indeed. Imagine: £864 to spend, with no need to act responsibly because – joy of joys – the same amount will turn up tomorrow, and the next day, and the next.

Except that we're not talking hypothetical, dreamland pounds and pennies here, but time. Real, actual time.

I wonder if we still feel as rich, then?

There are seasons when those seconds seem to zip past. At the end of the day, nothing much done. And, equally, how come at other times they drag by so slowly that I anticipate lunchtime at only half past ten?

I do know this, though: that if I had to choose between a fortune of time and a fortune of money, time would always win. In fact, there would be no real competition.

None of us know how much time on earth we have been allotted. It is one of God's mercies that we do not. If my days were numbered (and the number wasn't a big one), would I end up behaving like a wound-up toy: crazily, nonsensically active but not really going anywhere? Or, perhaps, would the converse be true: knowing I had oodles of time and ending up swanning around and wasting most of it?

This is where the truth of scripture can guide our hearts and our thinking. 'Hour by hour I place my days in your hand' isn't a bad motto. It's an even better prayer.

When hours are filled with the joy of creating,
Let's place them in his hand.

When time is stunted while we are waiting,
Let's place it in his hand.

When seconds drag and hours are long,
Let's place them in his hand.

When drowned by sorrow or filled with song,
Let's place them in his hand.

When time is short and the pressure is on,
Let's place it in his hand.

When time is up and a victory's won,
Let's place it in his hand.

Whenever, with whomever, for whatever,
Let's place time in his hand.

For he is our God, forever and ever,
And time is in his hand.

10

FACING FAILURE

'My sheep listen to my voice; I know them, and they follow me. I give them eternal life, and they shall never perish; no one will snatch them out of my hand.'
JOHN 10:27–28

'You have persevered and have endured hardships for my name, and have not grown weary.'
REVELATION 2:3

'His master replied, "Well done, good and faithful servant!"'
MATTHEW 25:21

*If I'm honest, I can find myself thinking of failure the entire
    time I'm creating.*
*Even when my heart is not only engaged but positively
    flying, when my hands and mind work in beautiful,
    peace-filled synchronicity – even then, I hear the
    voices:*
    It's bound to go wrong.
    What is it, anyway?
    I don't know why you're bothering.
    No one cares.
    Don't waste your time.
*I turn the radio up, hum a little louder, drown those
    naysayers out.*
But they still get in,
    find their ways through the cracks in my resilience,
    *picking – oh-so-gently at first – at my confidence until it
    lies in a crumbled heap at my feet.*
Creating is not hard.
*It was what I was born to do; it runs through my DNA
    as surely as the colour of my eyes.*
No, creating is not the problem.
*Perfectionism, though, might be, coupled with that
    curious tendency to overthink, to analyse, to squeeze
    the life out of it as fast as I'm trying to make it live.*

→

Lord, have mercy.
I am a self-fulfilling prophecy.
I take the words of those doom-filled voices and repeat
   them in my own voice.
They sound so utterly convincing when I do.
So, Lord, I'm turning these thoughts over to you.
I want to hear your voice, your kind, helpful, encouraging
   voice that speaks a better word into my soul.
Help me to trust you, Lord:
   trust that the dreams are in my heart because you put
      them there;
   trust that you can be my constant inspiration, strength
      and comfort;
   trust that what you have started, you will complete – in
      and through me.
Failure may continue to demand my attention;
   but you have my heart.

___

Prayers around facing failure

But he said to me, 'My grace is sufficient for you, for my power is made perfect in weakness.' Therefore I will boast all the more gladly about my weaknesses, so that Christ's power may rest on me. That is why, for Christ's sake, I delight in weaknesses, in insults, in hardships, in persecutions, in difficulties. For when I am weak, then I am strong.

2 CORINTHIANS 12:9–10

My flesh and my heart may fail, but God is the strength of my heart and my portion forever.

PSALM 73:26

Not only so, but we also glory in our sufferings, because we know that suffering produces perseverance; perseverance, character; and character, hope. And hope does not put us to shame, because God's love has been poured out into our hearts through the Holy Spirit, who has been given to us.

ROMANS 5:3–5

God, aware as I am of my own weakness and failures,
I want to thank you today that:
  you never fail;
  you never slumber nor sleep (Psalm 121:4);
  you never leave or forsake us (Hebrews 13:5);
  you are the same yesterday, today and forever (Hebrews
    13:8);
  you never do anything wrong.
You are always good, faithful and true.
You do not have off-days.
You never have moments when you are not in the mood.
You never walk away from your responsibilities.
Thank you.

Pause to reflect

Thank you that I can lean on you,
At all times and in all situations.
In the brokenness of disappointment,
  you are kind.
In the pain of rejection,
  you are compassionate.
In the frustration,
  you are my peace.
In the uncertainty,
  you are my safe place, my refuge.

Pause to reflect

→

Sovereign Lord, I give you my all,
  some of it in tiny shards.
Do with me what you will.
I trust you.
Amen.

———

God, I messed up today.
Just saying it out loud adds to the sense of shame.
It feels horrible.
Every instinct tells me to run and hide;
  to pretend it has not happened.
But why try to deny what you –
  at my side –
  have seen,
  every painful minute of it?
I'm hurting and so I come
  to the only one who can make anything better.
It is too soon to pick myself up,
  dust myself off and start again.
I need to sit among the debris for a while
  and just think.
Would you be my companion in that, please?
Hold my hand.
I don't want to feel alone in this.
Thank you, Lord.
Amen.

———

God, help me to remember today
  that failure is not the same as sin.
The feelings of self-condemnation
  threatening to overwhelm me
  warn me I have lost perspective,
  got things out of proportion.
This 'disaster' is not a blockage between us.
Hallelujah!
My flawed humanity has already received salvation.
Wonderful Jesus!
Even if my work cannot be redeemed,
  I can rejoice that I have been.
Thank you, Lord, for creating me
  as a 'human being'
  and not a 'human doing'.
Even on my worst days,
  you still love me utterly and completely,
  though I cannot love myself right now.
My limitations have left me frustrated,
  despondent.
So, please help me to remember
  that failure is not the same as sin –
  but even if it were,
  I have Jesus.
He is enough.
Yes and amen.

___

God, I wonder what creating was like for you?
Have you ever called something into being
    then regretted how it turned out?
Tragically, your word tells me that is so;*
    and therefore you understand
    when my own creations go wrong.
As if disappointment was not enough,
    I am my own judge,
        jury,
        executioner;
    berating myself for my failure.
But there is more.
Since it all went wrong,
    I have been trashing not only my work
    but myself.
In a breath, my mistake went
    from 'fixable' to 'disastrous';
    my cries of 'This is rubbish'
    changed to 'I am rubbish'.

→

Even saying it is painful.
I have fallen into a pit of despair,
  its sides greasy with hopelessness.
What do you think of it, Lord?
Do you share my opinion?
Is it really as terrible as I believe?

Pause to reflect

Be still, my soul, and wait for the Lord.
Remember he is good,
  all the time.
I choose to agree.
Amen.

*Genesis 6:6

_____

11

GETTING FINISHED

'It is finished!'

These were not only the triumphant last words of Jesus on the cross, but mine whispered into the air one night in March 1996. They were directed at a particularly complicated embroidery which I had hung that day, having spent three difficult years working on it. My words had even more significance than I realised. This project had been the focus of my multiple-miscarriage-based grief and, now it was finally complete, there was more to be concluded. Unknown even to myself, I was pregnant. That picture still hangs in my lounge, and my son is now a grown man.

Getting to the end of a project is always significant in its own ways. Perhaps it is the first in a particular genre or creative form; or it represented a special challenge. Maybe you have made a piece for commemorative reasons or as a unique gift for a treasured someone. Yes, indeed, being able to see for real what has only existed in sketches or imagination is a deeply satisfying moment. But what about the journey? If the saying is right, that in itself can be more important than the destination.

Everything I have ever created, whether that's in tactile crafting or music or written word, has involved a journey of discovery. Sometimes it is the literal skill that I have developed, the techniques and what they have demanded of me physically, intellectually and emotionally. At other times, I have had to dig deep into myself to find the patience and stamina to deal with exacting clients and then call on supreme diplomatic skills when it comes to negotiating the bill! Being creative doesn't just mean that we make stuff. God is always working in us as we work-play, meaning that we are changed in the process.

However, let's not use 'the journey is the main thing' as an excuse to not finish. (That embroidery I described took so long to complete because I kept laying it aside in favour of something easier. I completed at least two other smaller projects in my 'waiting until I felt braver' times.) The hill might be a tough one to climb, but we don't get the view from the top if we don't get to the top. In fact, it's those harder metaphorical climbs that make finishing all the more satisfying. If you're struggling to keep going, my advice? Keep on keeping on.

Finally, there is one thing I have learned about finishing that I wish I'd appreciated sooner: always celebrate.

Sometimes the wins come easily. They are worth celebrating.

Sometimes they are hard-won, costly, soul-stretching. They are most definitely worth celebrating.

And whether your tipple is champagne or tea, and whether you are surrounded by cheering supporters or on your own, just make sure you celebrate.

Why?

When we celebrate, we are acknowledging:

- the importance of what we have achieved;
- the time and effort we have expended were not in vain;
- that God is good and faithful and worthy of praise;
- that stopping to rest and reflect and receive satisfaction is a God-given gift.

Here's to finishing!

THE
END

Prayers for finishing

For if you lay the foundation and are not able to finish it, everyone who sees it will ridicule you, saying, "This person began to build and wasn't able to finish."
LUKE 14:29–30

… being confident of this, that he who began a good work in you will carry it on to completion until the day of Christ Jesus.
PHILIPPIANS 1:6

And here is my judgement about what is best for you in this matter. Last year you were the first not only to give but also to have the desire to do so. Now finish the work, so that your eager willingness to do it may be matched by your completion of it, according to your means.
2 CORINTHIANS 8:10–11

He also made the pots and shovels and sprinkling bowls. So Huram finished all the work he had undertaken for King Solomon in the temple of the Lord.
1 KINGS 7:40

For an impending deadline

God, I'm in trouble!
Pressure is mounting from without and within to get on
*   with this,*
*   to get it finished.*
My eagerness at the beginning has given over to fear:
*   that there isn't enough time;*
*   that I will not have enough energy;*
*   that the ideas will dry up.*
Come, Lord.

Pause to reflect

I consciously bring to mind that you are eternal,
*   above all and in all.*
You are Lord of all and my times are in your hands.
You are Lord of all and the creator of all things.
You are Lord of all and the sustainer of all things.

Pause to reflect

→

My prayer is not that you wave a magic wand,
*   that I will wake and find it done, like in a fairy tale.*
I know this is down to me.
It will never get finished unless I do it;
*   but my strength is not sufficient.*
This pace is neither sustainable nor wise.
So I pray for a greater sense that I'm not alone,
*   that we're working in partnership.*
I pray I can lean on you,
*   and let you bear the project's weight and responsibility.*
Come, Lord.
As I sit with my hands open, please take the burden
*   from me;*
*   give me your promised easy yoke.*
Help me to trust that you have given me enough time.
Help me receive your peace as I continue to work;
*   let your wisdom draw me into rest when I need it.*
Together, Lord, and only together can we do this.
In anticipation of all you will do, I thank you.
Amen.

____

God, you are the Alpha and the Omega.
I acknowledge you as the starter,
    the one who inspires our beginnings,
    speaking to our hearts and feeding us
    dreams of what might be.
What hope!
What potential!
All glory to you!
But I come to you now as Omega, the finisher.
Can that be said of me
    when procrastination and fear restrain
    and the beautiful, embryonic beginnings remain
    stunted and unborn?
Omega, you.
Not brave enough, me.
God, how I need you.
I want to tune into your heart again, into who you are.
You do not tease us and then abandon us.
You do not let us give birth to wind
    (how your word makes us smile sometimes!).

→

In your rhythmic purpose,
   there is a time to start
   and a time to finish.
You are behind, in and through
   both ends of the process.
I want to be more like you, Lord the finisher.
I want you to help me bring this project to completion.
No more excuses.
No more avoiding.
I choose to look to you, God.
Draw me closer.
Let me see the finishing tape ahead of me
   and let us run together towards it.
Amen.

____

God, you declared 'It is good'
  at every stage of creation.
When the image in your head
  was outplayed,
  displayed,
  you were satisfied.
At the end, with new humankind to share it,
  you declared it 'very good'
  and settled back to rest.
I have a question, God.
Will that apply to me,
Here and now?
Does being made in your image
  extend so very far
  that I will finish my doing
  and not only know that 'It is done'
  but that 'It is good'?
I pray so.
I hope so.

→

I long that all my effort, my striving,
  my caring and my trying
  will bring satisfaction to my heart.
Perhaps my prayer should be that I see it as you do:
  through eyes of wonder and surprise,
  without the lens of doubt and certain disappointment.
Let the hope that buoyed me at the start
  be present at the finish
As I hear your words:
  'Well done!'
  'You were faithful!'
  'Enter into my rest!'
Let it be so.
Amen.

———

God, you did it!
You heard my desperate cries –
  ever louder through the sleepless nights –
  and you answered!
You saw my need, my helplessness,
  my doubts and my wavering,
  and you ran to help me.
I was the psalmist 'going down for the third time'*
  and you rescued me.
Hallelujah!
God, we did it!
You took my hands,
  quickened my steps,
  lifted me,
  held me,
  kept me standing.
Hallelujah!
I lay aside the 'What now?',
  the second guessing,
  the critical reaction,
  and embrace the 'It is finished.'
It is finished.
The work is done.
I am spent but satisfied.
Hallelujah!

*Psalm 69:2 (MSG)

——

12

FACING SUCCESS

Character focus
Bezalel and Oholiab, the tabernacle supremos

Then the Lord said to Moses, 'See, I have chosen Bezalel son of Uri, the son of Hur, of the tribe of Judah, and I have filled him with the Spirit of God, with wisdom, with understanding, with knowledge and with all kinds of skills – to make artistic designs for work in gold, silver and bronze, to cut and set stones, to work in wood, and to engage in all kinds of crafts. Moreover, I have appointed Oholiab son of Ahisamak, of the tribe of Dan, to help him. Also I have given ability to all the skilled workers to make everything I have commanded you.'

EXODUS 31:1–6

I find this portion of scripture fascinating. The context is the construction of the tabernacle, whose precise blueprint was delivered to Moses by God himself over the course of several chapters. I marvel afresh that God – who spoke into chaos and darkness and brought forth creation by his word – would choose to partner with humankind in executing his designs. The stakes were high. This was the place where God would dwell among his people, where sacrifices and worship were to be offered every single day. No wonder the details were so pin-point precise. People being charged with the responsibility of suitably honouring God? Almost unthinkable!

Of course, it wasn't just 'any people'. Look at the credentials of Bezalel, the man God appointed. I wish my crafting CV looked as impressive! His handiworks crossed a number of media, all of which require specialist training. This is a man – I'm guessing not a young one, unless he was an absolute prodigy – who has taken the painstaking time to develop his natural gifting into finely honed skill, and we know how long some techniques take to master. I can imagine the fruit of his labours being nothing short of exquisite.

Look again, though, and you'll notice that he is outstanding even before his craft skills are mentioned. He is the first person in the Bible to be described as filled with the Spirit of God. We should not allow our New Testament filter to diminish the significance of this detail. In later books of the Bible, we discover that the Spirit of God enables prophets to speak God's word incisively and equips judges to rule well. Here, Bezalel's anointing seems to be purposed specifically for his crafts-manship. Additionally, he is blessed with giftings of wisdom, understanding and knowledge. This is not a one-dimensional, single-focused man, but a real all-rounder – and with a heart for God and his ways.

We should not imagine that – even with all these skills and supernatural enabling – Bezalel could have managed his work-load alone. Perhaps we are blinkered by our own experience of having to work at our craft in isolation and solitude and simply consider it normal. But look at the passage again and see that not only did God create a team, but he gave Oholiab to be Bezalel's right-hand man: someone to help shoulder the burden, bounce ideas off, share encouragement, commiserate and celebrate with. They might have received the commission of a lifetime, but the responsibility of the burden was all God's.

- *What aspects of this passage struck you most powerfully?*
- *Are you challenged to work differently?*
- *If you are feeling weighed down by all that is on your plate, spend some time asking for God to intervene in a way that will bless you and others.*

Prayers around facing success

Then Moses said to him, 'If your Presence does not go with us, do not send us up from here. How will anyone know that you are pleased with me and with your people unless you go with us? What else will distinguish me and your people from all the other people on the face of the earth?'
EXODUS 33:15–16

'I know your deeds. See, I have placed before you an open door that no one can shut. I know that you have little strength, yet you have kept my word and have not denied my name.'
REVELATION 3:8

The crucible for silver and the furnace for gold, but people are tested by their praise.
PROVERBS 27:21

God, I come to you in awe-filled thanks today:
  my heart is bursting!
I am standing on the threshold of success –
  I know it! –
  and it's only by your leading,
  your grace,
  your enabling,
  that it is so.
My many anxious prayers
  have besieged your throne
  day and night.
You have seen my tears,
  my fears,
  my bravado slipping to expose the self-doubt
  that you knew all along.
How glorious that you came to my rescue!

Pause to reflect

I can scarcely believe the moment has come.
Things are about to change for me.
There will be fresh challenges,
  but we shall face them together.
I worship you, my rock and fortress.
Success may well be fleeting
  but I am eternally grateful
  that you remain the same:
  the underpinning and security of my life
  in all its seasons.
Amen.

———

God, people are talking about me:
  good things,
  things that not only encourage me
  and energise me
  but flatter, too.
This could be dangerous, Lord,
  and I need your protection.
Don't let all this go to my head,
  or let pride spoil this moment.
Keep me grounded, Lord;
  keep me humble.
Let the only praise that interests me
  be what I offer to you.
You have gifted me,
  empowered me,
  strengthened me,
  and now brought me to the attention of others.
I claim no credit for this
  but give all glory to you,
  now and evermore.
Amen.

_____

God, I have worshipped you
  for many facets of your character:
  your faithfulness,
  your saving grace,
  your compassion.
But now I am learning something new,
  something that hasn't quite applied before:
  the rewarder.
Surely you have seen my hard work,
  my unstinting hours,
  the rest I have denied myself
  the sacrifices I have made.
I have not done so to twist your arm
  or manipulate your kindness,
  but only in honour of you
  and the giftings you've entrusted to me.
Yet surely you have begun to bless me
  with success and favour;
  I hear your 'Well done' whispering into my soul.
Thank you, God, so faithful, so true.
You see the lowly state of your servants
  humbled before you
  and you delight to lift them up.
All you have done and continue to do
  is marvellous in my eyes.
I will sing of your goodness as long as I live.
Amen.

———

God, I am so grateful
  for all the friends,
  colleagues and co-workers
  who have travelled with me so far.
Thank you for placing them alongside me
  to encourage and learn from each other
  as we pursued our dreams.
I continue to pray for them,
  that they would keep going
  and not so much as hesitate in pursuit of their goals.
But I have achieved mine,
  at least this one in nearest reach.
Already I feel a sense of separation from these dear ones,
  as if I have broken rank
  and we are no longer quite on the same team.
God, please step in!
Let our bonds withstand this change.
Let pettiness and jealousy be overcome by love.
Let none of us behave in ways
  that threaten our relationship.
You are the giver of good gifts,
  and I'm trusting that what is good for me
  is also good for those on my team.
Let it be so, Lord.
Let this be a season of great blessing
  for all of us,
  at whatever stage.
Amen.

———

13

THE TEACHING PROCESS

'The student is not above the teacher, nor a servant above his master. It is enough for students to be like their teachers, and servants like their masters.'
MATTHEW 10:24–25

Then Paul said: 'I am a Jew, born in Tarsus of Cilicia, but brought up in this city. I studied under Gamaliel and was thoroughly trained in the law of our ancestors.'
ACTS 22:3

I'm no athlete, despite my long legs and physical determination, but I have taken part in a number of relay races in my time. Tense affairs they are: the success of the team entirely depending on you, or so it seems. You stand, already leaning forward in anticipation of launching yourself down the track, awaiting your turn. The crowd is cheering on the first teammate; you know it's only a matter of seconds before you will start to run, tentative, on high alert, reaching backwards for the baton that bears the sweat of your forerunner. One fumble, one mistiming, and the entire race is over, but you can't afford to think like that. All you know is that, when you've been passed the baton, you crack on with your own running.

I wonder who your crafting forerunners have been? No doubt they have come to mind as you read these thoughts. A teacher? An artist at work? Your gifted parents? For me, they include my three piano teachers, each contributing significantly to my development as a musician, never knowing – I suspect – that they were raising someone who would pass their baton on to pupils of my own.

As I trace the chain back through the years, I have a curious image in my head: the row of cut-out paper figures you get when you fold a sheet of paper into a concertina then snip, snip, snip away. (Even as I think about it, I sense my tongue poking between my teeth and a frown form a crease between my eyebrows, and I am six years old once more.) The hand of each wonky figure is holding that of the ones either side, their interconnection obvious.

Every pupil once had a teacher.

Every teacher has once been a pupil.

Every beginner is inspired by a skilled worker.

Every skilled worker inspires the onlooker.

Hand in hand, on the cycle goes; one generation to another.

It takes time for the baton we have been given to be comfortable in our own hands. The learning process can be cruel, unkind and one to be endured rather than enjoyed. The mistakes are hard to forgive in ourselves. The unfulfilled expectations can be wearying and the disappointments crushing to the soul. And yet, if we can subject ourselves to the discipline and apply ourselves for sufficient hours, the pain gives way to joy, and it is true to say that the learning experience itself – and who has ever really finished their education – can satisfy our hearts in unique ways.

Wonky we may be – student and tutor alike – but when we hold on to those connections (even when they are paper-thin) we find not just a baton has been passed but creative life itself.

Prayers for teachers and students

'And he has given both [Bezalel] and Oholiab son of Ahisamak, of the tribe of Dan, the ability to teach others.'
EXODUS 35:34

'As for me, far be it from me that I should sin against the Lord by failing to pray for you. And I will teach you the way that is good and right.'
1 SAMUEL 12:23

And the Lord's servant must not be quarrelsome but must be kind to everyone, able to teach, not resentful.
2 TIMOTHY 2:24

Being a teacher

God, thank you for all the ways
  I can express my creativity,
  and for the satisfaction and joy
  I receive through doing what I love.
I am truly blessed!
Thank you for calling me to teach –
  to pass on not just skills and techniques,
  but excitement and enthusiasm too.
I sense your anointing and your pleasure
  and am humbled and thankful that you chose me.
For the privilege of seeing you at work in my students,
  I thank you, Lord.
For the joy of witnessing moments of new-found clarity,
  I thank you, Lord.
For the relief of seeing you release them from creative
    blocks,
  I thank you, Lord.
For the wonder of watching new shoots of gifting emerge,
  I thank you, Lord.
Yours is the easy yoke and the light burden;
  let me never be tempted to do this in my way or in my
    own strength.
I'm so grateful for all those you have entrusted to me.
I give you all the glory.
Amen.

———

God, you are the giver of all good gifts
*   and the initiator of grace.*
In my core – the very heart of who I am –
*   I know I am nothing without you.*
Yet I find myself tempted to show off,
*   to flaunt my ability in front of my students.*
In my excitement, I forget my place,
*   daring to claim the credit*
*   for what your generosity and kindness alone has*
*   given me.*
I'm ashamed, Lord.
I confess I get impatient with their progress
*   and want to take over.*
Too many times, my pride pushes compassion aside.
Have mercy, Lord.

Pause to reflect

Help me to remember my own journey
*   of errors and mess and slow growth,*
*   confirming I have no right to feel arrogant or superior.*
Forgive me, God, as I once more humble myself
*   before you,*
*   remembering I am nothing without you*
*   and have so much still to learn.*
Fill me afresh with the Holy Spirit
*   so I may teach from your anointing*
*   and through your good grace.*
Amen.

_____

God, thank you for choosing me
  to lead this workshop.
I'm so grateful for the chance to encourage,
  motivate and inspire
  this group of eager learners.
Help me to pitch the material
  so that no one is bored or left behind.
Help me instinctively sense who might need extra support.
Help me demonstrate with patience and clarity;
  keep me from rushing ahead.
I pray for each attendee,
  that you would give them the desires of their heart.
Release new gifting within them, Lord;
  fill them with fresh anointing.
I pray that all fear and trepidation
  be gone in Jesus' name,
  and that in its place would spring love, joy and peace.
Birth new friendships within the group,
  not just new skills,
  for you are a people-centred God.
Bless each one who comes, Lord,
  and let that include me too.
For your glory, I pray.
Amen.

———

Having a teacher

God, thank you for helping me find my teacher.
What a Godsend they truly are!
Thank you for opening my eyes
  to how much I have to learn.
What a relief it is to admit my weakness
  before you and before others.

Pause for reflection

Thank you for their expertise.
Thank you for their determination,
  for their diligence in mastering their craft.
Thank you for their resilience
  in the face of great difficulty and challenge.
Thank you for their mistakes that I can learn from,
  avoiding the pain of making my own.
Thank you that I benefit from all they have experienced
  and endured.

Pause for reflection

Thank you for their generosity,
  the sharing of their time and talent.
Thank you for their patience and perseverance.
You are a good God,
  and you have shown it in giving me _____ [name].
Amen.

____

God, thank you that in your word
   Jesus is called teacher.
How I pray he would be mine
   in this class,
   right now!
I feel overawed by everyone else.
They all seem to understand
   and know each step of the process,
   but I'm stuck.
I need help, I really do,
   but I'm too anxious to ask.
Lord, come and ease my troubled mind and clenching
      stomach.
Give me your peace, I pray.
Let my teacher look my way and know instinctively to
      come near.
Until then, give me your wisdom, please.
Show me how to ask.
Then give me the courage to do so.
Amen.

——

God, I thank you so much for my skills group.
Joining them was the answer to many prayers,
   and I shall always be grateful.
Thank you for my fellow learners,
   who are already becoming friends.
Thank you for our teacher, _____ [name],
   who is opening up this unique world to me.
But I confess I'm feeling vulnerable.
You see how few people are here
   and how many are my fears.
Please don't let the class be axed.
There is no 'lack of interest' here!
This is our artistic lifeblood, our oxygen.
We cannot thrive without it.
Please don't let my lack of skill and experience be
      too obvious.
Please turn my insecurities into opportunities for growing.
I don't want to be a coward, nor to stay afraid.
Let this be a season that proves to be highly significant in
      my life.
Lord, you know my heart.
You know how I've trusted you in the past.
Please answer my prayers for all our sakes –
   and, as ever, for your glory, majestic King.
Amen.

_____

14

PRAYERS FOR CREATIVES

I took a good look at my hands today.

Not to wash them or rub in some hand cream or notice that my nails needed a trim.

I simply held them open, letting the thin winter sunlight bathe their skin.

Wrinkled, they are – a complex surface of tiny lines which, if I were to draw them, might prove my longest project yet.

Scarred, they are. Some wounds I remember, while others are collateral damage; friendly fire, if you will.

I continue to hold them open, not, as you might think, in anticipation of receiving something. (I smile to myself. If that were the case, they would be wider!) It is a gesture of thanksgiving, of gratitude, of utter amazement that these hands have proved capable of creating so much over the years.

These hands, these average human hands, have cooked and baked, played musical instruments, plastered ceilings, painted walls, built sandcastles, sewed clothes, knitted jumpers, cut shapes out of card and fabric, and fashioned imaginary people and places in words. There is more, much more, I could list.

At times – often very good times – these hands have been tools that were extensions of my heart. They have attempted to convey love, hope, joy and exuberance. But there are other times I need to confess to, times they have not been tools but weapons. They have not demonstrated goodness but have testified to my inner struggles as they reacted in anger or frustration.

Lord, have mercy.

And there's more to these hands, much more, when I consider whose hands they have held. Friends, lovers, children, parents. I wonder if my touch left as deep an impression on them as they did on mine.

As I continue to meditate, lost in thought and memories that have slipped an arm across my shoulders, I think of Jesus. His hands were not wrinkled, for old age was not his to know. They were scarred, though – first by the life of a workshop and then, much more, by the laying down of that life.

Can I imagine a more powerful demonstration of love? His hands stretched as far as they could go in a gesture of welcome that endured until the end. His hands are now not just 'pierced' as if they had received a mere pinprick, but run through with ironwork. And still these hands, now crushed and bloodied, continue to recreate, to restore, to give life.

How can it be that he would do so for my sake?

Could I envisage ever putting my own hands to such use?

I pause, leaving space for my tears.

Then I close my palms together and use them for what they do best.

I pray.

Prayers for artists and painters

He has made everything beautiful in its time. He has also set eternity in the human heart; yet no one can fathom what God has done from beginning to end.
ECCLESIASTES 3:11

A good name is more desirable than great riches; to be esteemed is better than silver or gold.
PROVERBS 22:1

Whatever you do, work at it with all your heart, as working for the Lord, not for human masters.
COLOSSIANS 3:23

God, I am flying!
My paintbrush the means of uplift,
    the colours the fuel of my energy.
I made a discovery as I work-played today –
    or perhaps you pointed it out.
I gasped at the sight:
    the way that stroke transformed
    what, I see now, had been dull
    (though, secretly, I had been content).
I am a traveller exploring new territory,
    a veritable moon-walker!
What marvel, mystery and miracle
    rolled into one!
Thank you,
    thank you,
        thank you,
    for colour and my relationship with it;
    for the joy and the thrill
    where sometimes there is pain and slog.
For the commission from you
    to live this life in this way.
You are an awesome God
    and I love you!
Amen.

―――

God, would you invade this space today?
Please be the fresh inspiration I need;
*   not a muse – a fickle imaginary friend –*
*   but a constant, rock-steady source of all abundant*
*   goodness.*
And grant me courage, too,
*   to be daring and experimental,*
*   when I prefer being safe.*
Let me hear your 'Well done'
*   or your 'Steady now',*
*   so that I tread new paths*
*   without completely losing my way.*
I do, though, pray I lose the restraints
*   that painful times have imposed on me.*
Those poor reactions,
*   those ugly comments,*
*   the blank looks that brought shame.*
Would you give me grace to bear those times
*   when my work is misunderstood?*
Help me to so know your guidance
*   that I can silence the critics –*
*   especially those in my head –*
*   and implicitly trust you're leading me*
*   into verdant, fruitful territory.*
Amen.

___

God, I'm no Rembrandt
  or Constable,
  Dalí or Monet.
I feel it is only you
  who knows my name,
  who recognises my style.
Is this always how it will be?
Is the best I can hope for
  that I become a posthumous hit?
Lord, I paint because I cannot NOT paint.
My studio is the only place I am fully alive,
  my art the reason I get up each morning,
  the very oxygen in my lungs.
But days like today I'm left wondering:
  is it worth it – this effort, this toil?
If fire roared through my collection,
  would the world notice its loss?
My mind is sore,
  my heart heavy.
God, would you come,
  your footsteps light,
  your touch on my arm gentle,
  and make me feel better?
Would you tell me you love it?
That you love me?
I think, then, I might just have strength
  to carry on.
Amen.

_____

Character focus
Joseph, the unseen carpenter

Make it your ambition to lead a quiet life: you should mind your own business and work with your hands, just as we told you.
1 THESSALONIANS 4:11

Do nothing out of selfish ambition or vain conceit. Rather, in humility value others above yourselves, not looking to your own interests but each of you to the interests of the others.
PHILIPPIANS 2:3–4

If I were to ask you what Jesus' father Joseph's occupation was, I would expect the easy answer 'carpenter'. But did you know that the Bible doesn't actually say he was? It is something we deduce instead from Jesus being described as the 'carpenter's son' (Matthew 13:55). This led me to consider the 'background crews', who diligently apply their craft in order for someone else to shine.

Thousands of creatives – with all their skills, craftsmanship and experience – work behind the scenes. Think of a movie: the cast list of maybe as many as 30 names is pathetically short compared to the sometimes hundreds of others who are named as part of the production team. While only a handful will get the accolades and the megabucks renumeration, without those individuals beavering away in the background, the movie would never make it to the screen. It extends more widely too. The ghost writer of a famous celebrity's autobiography or novel may not get so much as a mention on the inside cover, though they have done the vast majority – if not all – the work. The cook who prepares all the recipes for a chef's TV show only to have their name hidden somewhere in the credits. And that's to say nothing of the researchers and designers who get the ideas off the ground in the first place.

It takes a certain kind of grace to be behind the scenes. Some of us work in sectors where 'getting a name for ourselves' is all part of the process. It can be something we wrestle with in our own minds: we have a heart-desire to put God first and seek glory for his name, and yet the industry requires us to be personally known in order to promote that God-glorifying work among a wider audience. How do we achieve balance? How do we 'get it right'?

Micah 6:8 may hold a key: 'He has shown you, O mortal, what is good. And what does the Lord require of you? To act justly and to love mercy and to walk humbly with your God.' Humility is not greatly prized as a virtue in our culture, being seen as weakness or someone being a 'pushover'. However, no matter how great our talent or skill, we simply can't claim the credit when we rightly recognise that God blessed us with all of it in the first place. When we have this corrected perspective, we can hold our gifting lightly, in a posture of surrender, and let God use it as he will – which may well include doing so on others' behalf.

Prayers for those behind the scenes: production/design

Just as a body, though one, has many parts, but all its many parts form one body, so it is with Christ… But in fact God has placed the parts in the body, every one of them, just as he wanted them to be. If they were all one part, where would the body be? As it is, there are many parts, but one body.

1 CORINTHIANS 12:12, 18–20

God, as I pray about my day
* I have a clear picture in mind:*
* intricate machinery,*
* a maze of interlocking cogs,*
* of many different sizes.*
What perfect imagery
* to pray into!*
Without each cog –
* however tiny –*
* its beating heart would stop.*
Thank you for placing me and my skills
* precisely and carefully into place.*
As I spin round
* in all I have to do*
* let me fit perfectly*
* with everyone around me.*
Let me have no delusion
* over where and how I fit.*
I have no need of limelight
* or special notice.*
Let me only 'keep turning'
* and play my part*
* within this production.*
Amen.

____

God, thank you for gifting me
  generously with imagination.
I love living inside my head
  where your creativity inspires me
  and excites me.
Thank you that ideas come thick and fast
  from the tiniest of sparks.
I rejoice in my uniqueness.
Thank you for delivering me
  from the need to fit in,
  to conform.
I pray that you lead me in every step
  of development,
    that I resist the temptation to settle;
    that I neither over-simplify
    nor over-complicate.
Let my ideas translate into schemes and projects
  that have your life-breath in them.
Thank you for the tech at my disposal,
  but let my reliance be on you.
I pray your wisdom in communicating with others;
  that I pitch well – avoiding insult! –
  and that what results
  brings glory to your name.
Amen.

_____

Prayers for those in fashion/dressmaking

'And why do you worry about clothes? See how the flowers of the field grow. They do not labour or spin. Yet I tell you that not even Solomon in all his splendour was dressed like one of these.'

MATTHEW 6:28–29

God, thank you for clothing Adam and Eve
when they needed shielding from their shame.
Though their sin had marred your image in them,
and spoiled the 'very good' you had created,
you showed kindness and mercy
in ways they could understand.
As I seek to create clothing in this space,
whether for me or for one I may never meet,
may I work-play with compassion.
Let my clothing be a gift of grace
as well as covering,
of adornment
as well as function.
Anoint me with the skilful ability you demonstrate
all around me, in clothing nature.
You bestow beauty on the plants of field and garden,
woodland and coastline,
every leaf and petal bearing witness to your glory.
You did not restrict your colour palette
or curtail your love of variety,
any more than you withhold any blessing from us.
Let what I produce today be, therefore,
an act of generosity
and connection
as well as creation.
Amen.

———

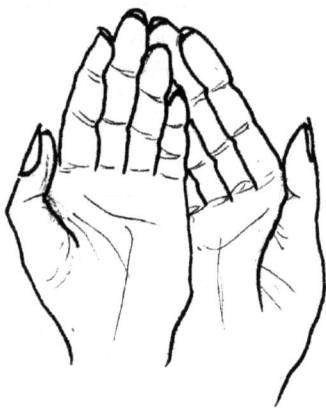

Prayers for food-crafters

When the dew was gone, thin flakes like frost on the ground appeared on the desert floor. When the Israelites saw it, they said to each other, 'What is it?' For they did not know what it was… The people of Israel called the bread manna. It was white like coriander seed and tasted like wafers made with honey.

EXODUS 16:14–15, 31

God, thank you that nothing you create is ordinary.
Even manna – so eluding description,
  so evading explanation –
  had the ethereal taste of heaven.
Help me remember with gratitude today
  your provision born of concern for our bodies,
  and your inimitable sense of fun
  in how you have supplied it.
Thank you that the heaven-on-earth garden of Eden
  held a feast not just for bodies
  but for eyes;
  help me, today, to keep that heavenly focus.
I bear the responsibility, it feels,
  for other people's celebrations.
My creations form the centrepiece,
  set the tone,
  establish the memories.
I need to get it right!
Help me to have a steady hand
  and unwavering focus.
Let all my equipment serve me well
  and be under my tight control.
Keep me alert to your promptings
  so that I know when to stop
  and when to add more detail.
Give me wisdom over which battles to fight
  and which to let go.
Above all, I seek to glorify you
  and honour those I am serving.
In Jesus' name I pray,
Amen.

____

Prayers for glassworkers

The wall was made of jasper, and the city of pure gold, as pure as glass… The twelve gates were twelve pearls, each gate made of a single pearl. The great street of the city was of gold, as pure as transparent glass.

REVELATION 21:18, 21

God, the ancient glassware of generations past,
  in windows,
  utensils,
  jewellery and ornament,
  reminds me that my work carries legacy.
Thank you that it is worth it –
  all the pain,
  all the failures,
  all the frustration.
That sand can become such treasure
  is one of your special miracles
  and I am blessed indeed to share in it.

Pause to reflect

God, would you help me today
  in every stage of every process?
Give strength to my body
  and focus to my mind.
Keep me from harm
  as I dare to experiment.
Let me be dazzled afresh by colour and form,
  ever in awe of what this speaks of you
  and the heavens in which you dwell,
glorious Lord!
Amen.

———

Prayers for illustrators

Open my eyes that I may see wonderful things in your law.
PSALM 119:18

God, thank you for giving me eyes to see
beyond the natural,
translating ideas into art-form.
Thank you for the daily visual delight
of my imagination
birthing new ways of seeing the world –
and, indeed, whole new worlds!
As I work-play today,
I ask that you sanctify my thoughts,
nudging me when I'm tempted to veer off
and miss the perfect way forward.
I know the impact my work can have.
Let the messages I present
be ever God-pointing,
God-honouring,
God-glorifying.
Amen.

_____

God, what joy and privilege it is
  to decorate the written work of others.
Thank you for choosing me
  to collaborate with other creatives.
Let those relationships be sweet
  and successful, I pray.
Give me wisdom and clarity of mind
  in interpreting their words,
    that I enhance their meaning
    and don't detract from their own beauty.
Let what we create
  be far and above
  the sum of their parts.
Amen.

———

God, my prayer today is for work
beyond this current project.
Even as I approach the middle stages
I'm aware of fear creeping up on me,
whispering that this may be it.
What would I do
if the work dried up?

Pause to reflect

Your word springs to mind
and becomes my prayer:
'Because of the Lord's great love
we are not consumed,
for his compassions never fail.
They are new every morning;
great is your faithfulness.'*
I choose to trust in your goodness,
in your provision.
Let my reputation grow, Lord,
as well as my reliance on you.
My hand in yours,
lead me on.
Amen.

*Lamentations 3:22–23

_____

Prayers for leatherworkers

Everyone who had blue, purple or scarlet yarn or fine linen, or goat hair, ram skins dyed red or other durable leather brought them.

EXODUS 35:23

God, there are so many ways
  I could thank you
  for creating animals.
Through them you have given humankind
  companions and workers.
As food sources they nourish us,
  heart, soul and body,
  and I am grateful.
But I thank you especially
  for the gift of animal skin
  and the delight of working with it.
Thank you that each one is unique,
  each defect and blemish a testimony
  to the life this pelt contained.
As I work-play today,
  I honour before you this precious creature!
I want to thank you, too,
  for those involved in this leather's processing –
  especially if they were employed in difficult
    circumstances.
Help me not to be careless
  with knife, stitch or glue.
May my sweat – gladly spent on my craft! –
  not stain or spoil.
May what I produce be beautiful in its usefulness
  and give glory to you.
Amen.

———

Character focus
Hiram, the 'mere' bronze-sculptor

> But who is able to build a temple for him, since the heavens, even the highest heavens, cannot contain him? Who then am I to build a temple for him, except as a place to burn sacrifices before him? Send me, therefore, a man skilled to work in gold and silver, bronze and iron, and in purple, crimson and blue yarn, and experienced in the art of engraving, to work in Judah and Jerusalem with my skilled workers, whom my father David provided.
>
> 2 CHRONICLES 2:6–7

We have already met Bezalel and Oholiab, the master craftsmen who worked on the Mosaic tabernacle. Generations have gone by, and now Solomon is planning to build a temple of epic proportions for the worship of his glorious God. It is a plan that had its roots in his father, David, who was told clearly that it was not his to build, but his son's (see 2 Samuel 7:12–13). Now the time has come, and our verses today show both Solomon's misgivings at the enormity of the task and his iconic wisdom in executing it.

Enter Hiram, hired directly by Solomon himself, head-hunted and literally shipped in from Tyre to join the team who would fit out the temple in incredibly elaborate style. Confusingly, he bears the same name as his king and, even more so, is sometimes misnamed as Huram Abi within the Bible passages. (Who hasn't committed that kind of *faux pas* at one time or another?)

We know that he was the son of a widow, his late father having been a coppersmith, and his speciality was working in bronze. When we read the whole account and discover the massive volume of gold deployed in the project, it might seem that to be a mere bronze worker was a bit of a come-down. But let's read on…

The two bronze pillars he fashioned were 18 cubits high – that's 8.23 metres in today's money. I suspect most people would be too over-awed by the almost 5 metre circumference to bother looking up; but, if they did, they would notice that on the capitals of the columns (which added a further 2.28 metres to their height) were 'nettings of latticework and twisted threads of chain work' (1 Kings 7:17, TLV) and, moreover, on that netting were two rows of pomegranates, all set on a lily design.

Next, the Bible tells us, he:

> … made the Sea of cast metal, circular in shape, measuring ten cubits across from rim to rim and five cubits high. It took a line of thirty cubits to measure round it. Below the rim, figures of bulls encircled it – ten to a cubit. The bulls were cast in two rows in one piece with the Sea.
> The Sea stood on twelve bulls, three facing north, three facing west, three facing south and three facing east. The Sea rested on top of them, and their hindquarters were towards the centre. It was a handbreadth in thickness, and its rim was like the rim of a cup, like a lily blossom. It held 3,000 baths.
> 2 CHRONICLES 4:2–5

The sheer scale of Hiram's work is staggering. That bronze 'sea', just described, contained enough water to fill 2,000–3,000 baths – about 66,000 litres – and yet it was no utilitarian project. Once more, we read of lily petals, along with vast statues of bulls.

This was a man who believed in going the extra distance.

Why would he spend (waste?) so much time, effort, and material creating something that couldn't easily be seen with the naked eye?

We, as Christian creatives, know the answer only too well: because excellence mattered to him; because his God was worthy of such lavishness; because to give less than his all would have been to dishonour both himself and God.

That's why we work so hard, even when no one notices.

We cannot not do so.

Prayers for metalworkers

God, you did not limit yourself
  but outworked your creativity
  through every medium,
  each atom of raw material,
  a mine of potential.
I remind myself today
  that I am handling what you have already touched.
You wove seams of treasure
  within the hidden depths of landscape,
  weaving me, too, in different ways
  knowing that there would come a day –
  today! –
  when these two elements of your creation
  would unite in glorious synergy.

→

So as I cast and hammer,
chase and solder,
let praise arise that you have chosen me
for the awesome privilege
of partnering with you, God,
master crafter.
Let worship take my creating
to the heights of your throne room
where I kneel, as once Magi did,
and present it at your feet;
grateful, so heartfelt grateful
for it all.
Amen.

____

God, I love that you are not a God of the plain,
  the merely functional.
You delight in lavishing intricate detail
  throughout your world,
  even where it may not be noticed.
Let my creations have that sense
  of 'above and beyond'.
Let me not settle for 'enough'
  as I seek to emulate your ways.
I pray for those who will one day
  wear my jewellery,
  embellishing with my humble offerings
  the beauty you have already bestowed.
Guide me, inspire me,
  keep my motivation pure,
  that the focus remains on you:
  the one whose perfection needs no adornment.
Amen.

———

Character focus
David, the anointed

Saul's attendants said to him, 'See, an evil spirit from God is tormenting you. Let our lord command his servants here to search for someone who can play the lyre. He will play when the evil spirit from God comes on you, and you will feel better.' So Saul said to his attendants, 'Find someone who plays well and bring him to me.' One of the servants answered, 'I have seen a son of Jesse of Bethlehem who knows how to play the lyre. He is a brave man and a warrior. He speaks well and is a fine-looking man. And the Lord is with him'... Whenever the spirit from God came on Saul, David would take up his lyre and play. Then relief would come to Saul; he would feel better, and the evil spirit would leave him.

1 SAMUEL 16:15–18, 23

At this stage of his life, David is still a shepherd boy in charge of his father Jesse's flocks. Samuel has plucked him from obscurity to anoint him as the next king, following God's rejection of King Saul. With his coronation still some way off, he remains very much in the background of the main action. But just as God saw him and chose him when everyone else around him was dismissing him as irrelevant, so, too, his musical talent – perhaps more usually having sheep for an audience – has not gone unnoticed.

Saul was not a stable man. The Bible describes him suffering volatile, violent mood swings that no one can appease. No one, that is, except David.

I wonder if you relate to any of this today? Perhaps you have been grafting away in the background for a very long time, while others around you seem to stand head and shoulders taller and gain all the success. You continue to beaver away, telling yourself that the most important thing is how valuable your creativity is to you, even if no one ever notices who you are or what you do.

But here's the thing: God sees you. You are not invisible to him. More than that, he sees right into your heart. He has seen when it has rejoiced at a win – however big or small – and when it has grieved in dark days of failure or disappointment. Nothing you have done behind the scenes has gone unnoticed by our loving Father.

Have you spotted, too, that it wasn't just David's skill that was being deployed, but his anointing? After listing his attributes of skilful lyre playing, bravery, eloquence and handsome features, we read the simple phrase: 'And the Lord is with him.'

A very long time ago, someone once told me, 'One plus God is a majority.' We must never underestimate the value or significance of God being with us.

May he bless you today with his presence, anointing and deep soul-satisfaction.

Prayers for musicians/song-writers

Sing to him a new song; play skilfully, and shout for joy.
PSALM 33:3

They held harps given them by God and sang the song of God's servant Moses and of the Lamb: 'Great and marvellous are your deeds, Lord God Almighty. Just and true are your ways, King of the nations.'
REVELATION 15:2–3

Songwriting

God, before a song comes from my mouth
  let it be sung in worship from my heart.
Before the words have formed on my tongue,
  let my thoughts have come through the fire,
  refined, purified,
  worthy of you.
Let each word be paired with sound
  so precisely,
  so sublimely,
  that their heavenly origin
  be unmistakeable.
Speak through each syllable,
  echo through each phrase,
  O living word.
Open my ears to hear you
  in each note I sing and play,
  taking me deeper into your heart
  and conveying more of you
  to a needy world.
Amen.

———

Composition

God of all the senses,
   Master and Lord of each emotion,
   let my ears and heart be enthralled by you today.
Stir my auditory senses,
   both external and internal,
   to be in complete alignment with your prompting.
Your word tells me you sing over me.
I pray that I would hear those sounds,
   receive what they convey,
   and translate them into what I create.
Let me not be swayed by the tunes of others,
   distracting me into their well-worn groove.
Lead me on a musical path as yet less travelled
   but which many may follow.
Come, Holy Spirit,
   infuse all I compose with the essence of God
   to glorify him and stir his people.
Amen.

———

Prayers for papercrafters

This is the day that the Lord has made; let us rejoice and be glad in it.
PSALM 118:24 (ESV)

And he said: 'Truly I tell you, unless you change and become like little children, you will never enter the kingdom of heaven.
MATTHEW 18:3

God, thank you that you welcome children,
* applauding their playfulness,*
* their love of exploring,*
* their sense of fun.*
With scissors in hand
* I feel like a child again today,*
* loved and understood.*
My hopes may no longer be for a snowflake
* or that my row of hand-holders*
* would remain intact when they unfurl;*
* but a sense of wonder remains*
* at the intricacy borne from simplicity.*
Invade my nervousness, Lord,
* infusing it with anticipation*
* and not fear.*
Steady my fingers,
* slow my breathing,*
* give me peace-filled confidence*
* that each fold,*
*   each snip*
* would be perfectly placed.*
Let my concentration not wander.
Keep my eyes as sharp as my tools.
Draw me into pausing
* whenever I'm tempted to rush;*
* and let me sense your pleasure*
* as we discover together what I have made.*
All glory to you!
Amen.

———

God, I thank you for the blank page,
   this pristine sheet
   imprinted with possibilities.
It lies flat now,
   its contours as limited as this tabletop,
   yet my inner eye already
   sees it morphing into shape.
My fingers are twitching to get folding,
   my mind one, two, three steps ahead,
   as my heartbeat quickens.
Steady me, God,
   let me feel your hand on my shoulder
   staying my too-eager hands.
Remind me to never lose sight of accuracy –
   you know how I can get carried away –
   so that nothing spoils the process.

→

Help me not be disappointed;
  my own standards are too high.
I pause to consider your perfection.
How awesome is every detail you made!
Not an atom is out of place!
What glory there is in that perfection alone,
  what breathtaking wonder!
Call me higher, Lord,
  beyond my capabilities
  and restrictions.
Expand my vision,
  increase my skills.
I want to be more like you!
Let your presence run like a watermark
  through this paper creation today.
Amen.

_____

God, thank you for paper.
  not the bleached, machine-rolled,
  generic, ordinary kind –
  though prized for what it conveys;
    but hand-picked,
    hand-pressed,
    hand-made.
This, this is a work of art:
  beauty in its very form.
I love the rawness combined with refinement
  that reminds me of its origins.
I relish the feel of it,
  the coarseness of the fibres
  derived from plants of your making.
A petal, a leaf,
  immortalised within the pulp:
  nature arrested.

→

I stroke over my damp brush;
  the colour deepens,
  intensifies,
  waiting for the moment
  when I begin to tear –
  no violent act but one of surrender,
  the fibres parting as close friends might:
  with reluctance but no pain.
God, may I learn from this paper
  your work in me:
  how you hand-select the elements
  and position them just so,
  so that when I am pressed and crushed,
  squeezed and torn,
  I am ever more beautiful,
  ever more useful to the master.
Amen.

———

Prayers for performing artists

You have searched me, Lord, and you know me… Where can I go from your Spirit? Where can I flee from your presence?
PSALM 139:1, 7

'A good tree cannot bear bad fruit, and a bad tree cannot bear good fruit… Thus, by their fruit you will recognise them.'
MATTHEW 7:18, 20

God, thank you for calling me to work-play
  within the performing arts industry,
  where I am free to express myself
  and be who I was created to be.
Though I may be 'behind a mask',
  let me never feel I am hiding from you.
I thank you that I never need
  to pretend in your presence,
  for you see me, through and through.
I pray for my Christian witness
  in this arena marked by superficiality.
May my love for you be seen in my work,
  that my performances have a deep effect on the
    audience.
Let the message linger long after curtain call.
Have your way, God!
Meet the needs of this hungry, love-starved world,
  using me – even me!
  for Jesus' sake,
Amen.

_____

God, thank you for giving us ways to communicate
  without words,
    beyond speech.
I thank you for my fellow musicians,
  who touch souls that are jaded and weary;
    bring ease to ears that have heard too much yet not
      enough.
Let those who listen find peace in place of striving,
  invigoration instead of apathy.
Let them hear the voice of the Father
  singing over them.
I thank you for dancers,
  whose moves – though disciplined and controlled –
  speak so eloquently of freedom.
Stir us up, Lord!
Shake us from our passivity
  through these God-ordained arts!
You are Lord of all:
  body, soul and spirit.
Release your Spirit in us, your chosen ones
  that we exercise our gifting under your anointing
  and minister restoration to those who look on.
Amen.

———

God, I pray for my body today,
that it would be equal to the demands made of it.
Thank you for my health,
that daily gift of grace
that enables me to exercise my creativity.
Remind me, Lord, that I am not a machine;
prompt me to rest and care for myself
in line with your word.
I pray not just for physical stamina
but mental resolve
to remember all that I have rehearsed.
Let my mood be sweet,
my temperament even,
whatever happens.
In all these things,
may your holy name be honoured.
Amen.

———

Prayers for perfumers

Make these into a sacred anointing oil, a fragrant blend, the work of a perfumer. It will be the sacred anointing oil.
EXODUS 30:25

While he was in Bethany, reclining at the table in the home of Simon the Leper, a woman came with an alabaster jar of very expensive perfume, made of pure nard. She broke the jar and poured the perfume on his head.
MARK 14:3

God, I am in awe of your gift of fragrance,
  to my mind the pinnacle of creation!
That something invisible could make itself so powerfully
    known
  speaks so much of you and your ways!
Would you sanctify my work-play today,
  imbue it with that sense of the sacred
  once reverenced by your servants, the priests?
Guide my senses today –
  harnessed with an awareness of your presence –
  so I may work with skill and precision,
  blending and shaping in complete synergy.
Let me never underestimate the effects of my perfume
  on mind,
    body,
      soul.
I pray that you would minister through my products
  gifts of grace and healing,
  restoration, peace and well-being.
May my highest goal be to bear the fragrance of Christ
  and share it with others.
Amen.

_____

Prayers for photographers

God saw all that he had made, and it was very good.
GENESIS 1:31

'Listen to this, Job; stop and consider God's wonders.'
JOB 37:14

Landscape

God, I stand awestruck by this landscape you have
  created.
What majesty!
What vastness!
My eyes are captivated by your glory
  radiating from every element.
How can I possibly frame such a vista
  or distil into pixels
  all that you're revealing in front of me?
I am mesmerised into inaction,
  humbled into reverence.

Pause to reflect on God's glory

→

Since a miracle was needed to bring all of this into being,
  I pray for a miracle to capture it.
Help me, God, choose the precise moment to shoot –
  when the light, so constantly changing, is at its most
    sublime.
Open my eyes yet wider,
  infuse my instincts with your wisdom,
  to know when the moment is 'now'.
I pray that my images might somehow display
  more than my eyes have noticed.
Then do another miracle,
  through the image itself,
  that this 2D representation becomes more than alive
  to those who have never been here
  and yet will somehow see.
Amen.

———

Portrait

God, I thank you for this person before me,
  that you declared their creation 'very good'.
Let there be a sense today
  that it is you behind the lens,
  directing the shot,
  helping me see as you see.
Break through the limits of my equipment
  so I may capture not only
  the glory of their physical form
    but something of their inner beauty too.
Increase my skill;
  manage their expectation!
Let the results bring joy to their face
  and to your heart.
Amen.

Prayers for potters

Yet you, Lord, are our Father. We are the clay, you are the potter; we are all the work of your hand.
ISAIAH 64:8

So I went down to the potter's house, and I saw him working at the wheel. But the pot he was shaping from the clay was marred in his hands; so the potter formed it into another pot, shaping it as seemed best to him.
JEREMIAH 18:3–4

God, master potter,
   the first to see that the dust of the earth –
   mere sweepings to our untrained eye –
   could become clay to house your very image,
   remind me today that your work is not done.
For us, your precious people,
   the ways of creation were not sufficient.
Life-containing is your breath
   and all-powerful is your word
   and yet…
You chose to form us by hand,
   delighting to leave your fingerprints on us.
How I need your touch today!
Let me yield afresh to your moulding of my life.
Let me not resist you
   (as if I am perfect already!),
   but rather submit to your kneading,
   painful though it may be.
As I wrestle with lumpen clay today,
   may I sense you working on me,
   for your glory.
Amen.

────

God, I need you.
I love being a potter – following in your footsteps! –
  but it is so hard.
I pray you would strengthen my body;
  take away the stresses and strains
  in my hands, wrists and back.
Keep me calm, Lord,
  so I don't panic
  when it all takes longer than I think.
Help me not to rush –
  I don't want to mess this up! –
  but infuse me with patience and peace.
Let the glazing go well, please!
I've worked so hard,
  got so far;
  but if the colour is not right,
    if…
    if…
Be Lord of my equipment, I pray.
Let everything work as it should
  and… God?
Please don't let it crack as it fires,
  or let me drop it!
So much is at stake here;
  you know how important all this is to me.
Please come through for me, God,
  the master potter.
Amen.

____

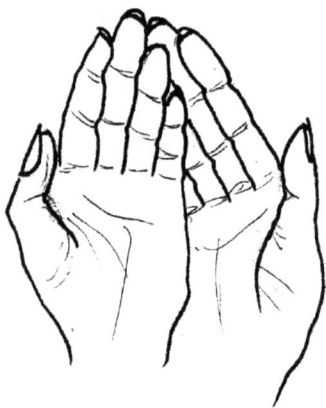

Prayers for restorers

The king and Jehoiada gave [a great amount of money] to those who carried out the work required for the temple of the Lord. They hired masons and carpenters to restore the Lord's temple, and also workers in iron and bronze to repair the temple.

2 CHRONICLES 24:12

Your people will rebuild the ancient ruins and will raise up the age-old foundations; you will be called Repairer of Broken Walls, Restorer of Streets with Dwellings.

ISAIAH 58:12

'Forget the former things; do not dwell on the past. See, I am doing a new thing! Now it springs up; do you not perceive it? I am making a way in the wilderness and streams in the wasteland.'

ISAIAH 43:18–19

God, I can start my day in no other way
  than to thank you, in profound gratitude,
  not just for creating me –
  though that would be praiseworthy enough –
  but for seeing my pitiful state
  and restoring me.
You took what the world saw as bearing little value.
You picked up not just me as I am
  but the scattered pieces of who I have been –
  reminders too sharp for me to hold,
  fragments too broken to be of use.
The cliché speaks truth: that, in your economy,
  nothing is wasted.
No second has passed when you were not active in and
    around me.

→

No opportunity has been missed that you cannot replay.
No tear has fallen to the ground
* but you have caught each one,*
* preserved them in a jar;*
* savoured,*
* cherished as holy,*
* each expression of my breaking heart.*
Is this why you called me to partner with you
* in this boundless work of grace?*
The restored becoming the restorer?
The passion in my heart not to somehow airbrush the past
*   – as if that could even be so –*
* but to rescue from life's ravages.*
I follow humbly in the footsteps of the Master Restorer,
* bringer of new life to objects and his subjects.*
In Jesus' name,
Amen.

_____

God, as ever, I bring my work to you today;
  not just the object on my bench
  but the one who has brought it.
Their story tugged at my heart,
  my only response a willing urge
  to help, to put things right.
How much more do you love them!
How deeply you have felt their pain,
  sorrow,
    disappointment!
As I work, in painstaking detail,
  I pray for steady hands,
  an incisive mind,
  and unwavering focus.
May I not create more damage,
  however unwitting.
Let my touch be light enough that
  I honour the original maker
  as well as the owner.
Hold us all with tenderness.
This matters, God.
Amen.

———

God, you see all things,
  both hidden and exposed.
You see the damage that is undeniable
  and that which is yet to be uncovered.
You discern which cause was accident
  and which was malicious,
  and through your grace, forgiveness and mercy,
  it matters not how harm was done.
Even as I conduct each process,
  I sense your call to look up,
    ahead,
      beyond.
'Forget the past,' you say,
  in words of firm compassion.
A new day is coming.
Dead bones can live again.
Sin is defeated.
Hallelujah!
Let this truth ring clear over me today:
  the past does not have the final word.
Amen.

———

Prayers for sculptors

Then the Lord God formed a man from the dust of the ground and breathed into his nostrils the breath of life, and the man became a living being.
GENESIS 2:7

'Is not my word like fire,' declares the Lord, 'and like a hammer that breaks a rock in pieces?'
JEREMIAH 23:29

God, the first sculptor,
  who fashioned humankind from clay,
  I come to you in awe
  and with thanksgiving.
Awe that creation is filled with sculptural majesty
  and thanks that I can follow in your footsteps.
Watch over my body, I pray,
  as I work-play today,
  that my hands remain steady,
  my eyes centred and focused
  and my breathing calm.
Let my movements be measured,
  my touch precise.
Remind me to step back,
  to walk away
  and recalibrate my perspective.
Let me see as you see!
Let my creations not be pale imitations
  of what you have already made,
  but living representations
  declaring my unique take on the world.
Show me when to stop,
  when to say 'Enough!'
  and let me hear your 'Well done'
  as I gratefully take my rest.
Amen.

———

God, thank you for this stone
  that has been centuries in the making –
  each strata telling a story
  I was not present to hear.
What privilege it is to handle it,
  respectful of its lifting from the ground
  for such a time as this.
Let my preparation be adequate,
  my drawings acting as a compass
  as I set to with my chisel.
Let me not push this stone to its limits
  and bemoan that it has broken.
Instead, let me notice the points of weakness
  and respect them –
  as you do in me.
Let the care I take today
  remind me of your touch in my life:
  chipping away what is hiding my truest form,
  revealing the beauty only you can now see.
Speak your life
  through this inanimate block
  and turn the hearts of those who see it
  to you,
  in praise of your glory.
Amen.

———

Character focus
Paul, the jobbing tentmaker

> After this, Paul left Athens and went to Corinth. There he met a Jew named Aquila, a native of Pontus, who had recently come from Italy with his wife Priscilla, because Claudius had ordered all Jews to leave Rome. Paul went to see them, and because he was a tentmaker as they were, he stayed and worked with them.
> ACTS 18:1–3

Not all creatives execute their art and craft for its aesthetic charm. While some are able to weather the economic implications of choosing heart over reason, others have no choice but to earn a living. Somehow. Anyhow.

It can be a constant balancing act. How do we satisfy the inner desire to create with the need to pay the bills? Can the two be reconciled?

To use Paul as an example might seem off the mark; after all, he was an apostle, not a craft-worker. But his ministry, to which he was devoted with single-minded focus, required him to labour for little financial reward. He was certainly choosing 'heart' (largely because he had surrendered it to Christ on the Damascus Road) over hard currency. Having friends who could put him up when he travelled was a plus, for sure, but his living costs were hardly low. Conservative estimates for how much it actually cost him to write his first letter to the Corinthians come out at around £1,600 in today's money – and that does not include the travel costs of Titus in delivering it. We know, too, from what he wrote to the Ephesian church that he was keen to pay his own way wherever possible:

> I have not coveted anyone's silver or gold or clothing. You yourselves know that these hands of mine have supplied my own needs and the needs of my companions. In everything I did, I showed you that by this kind of hard work we must help the weak, remembering the words the Lord Jesus himself said: 'It is more blessed to give than to receive.'
> ACTS 20:33–35

Paul hailed from Cilicia, which was famous for the quality of its goats-hair cloth – largely used in tent-making. We might understand from the scriptures that Paul's upbringing was heavily weighted in education: he studied to a high level and he learned from the best. However, we also know that it was standard practice for a Jewish rabbi to learn a trade. In Paul's case, he probably sewed lengths of cloth together and attached the ropes and loops.

It was not 'crafting for a living' in the idyllic way we might dream of, but his skills provided much-needed income which enabled him to keep doing what he knew he should – and to help his fellow travellers out, too.

No doubt he was able to apply his own words to the situation: 'I know what it is to be in need, and I know what it is to have plenty. I have learned the secret of being content in any and every situation, whether well fed or hungry, whether living in plenty or in want. I can do all this through him who gives me strength' (Philippians 4:12–13).

Crafting is often put into the category of 'bringing its own reward.' When it actually earns us some money, it is blessing indeed.

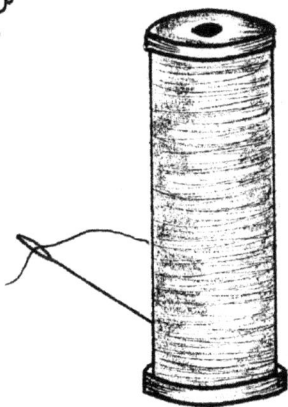

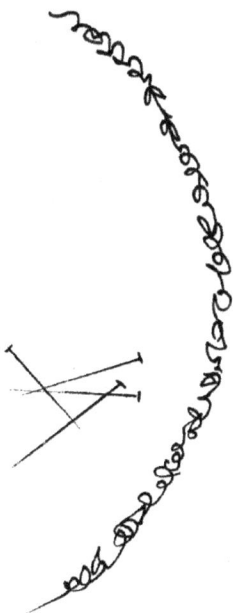

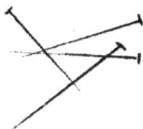

Prayers for textile-workers

For you created my inmost being; you knit me together in my mother's womb. I praise you because I am fearfully and wonderfully made; your works are wonderful, I know that full well. My frame was not hidden from you when I was made in the secret place, when I was woven together in the depths of the earth.

PSALM 139:13–15

'The grass withers and the flowers fall, but the word of our God endures forever.'

ISAIAH 40:8

Yet this I call to mind and therefore I have hope: Because of the Lord's great love we are not consumed, for his compassions never fail.

LAMENTATIONS 3:21–22

God, I bring my worship to you, Lord of all the senses.
You gave sight, that we would delight in you through our
*   eyes;*
* hearing, that we would thrill at the sound of your voice;*
* taste, that we would enjoy your goodness;*
* smell, that we would bear your fragrance;*
* and touch, that we would know the satisfaction of*
*   connection.*
As I work-play today,
* may I know the joy of my senses engaging*
* in service of your glory.*
May my fingers be dextrous as I weave my yarn,
* may my skills increase in each familiar movement.*
May I understand what 'seamless' truly means
* as my hands synergise with what I am crafting.*
May I be aware of your touch on me,
* grateful for all you are creating in me.*
May moments of monotony drift my thoughts towards you
* and fill my tired mind with worship.*
Creator God,
* master weaver,*
* worthy of all praise,*
* now and always,*
Amen and amen.

———

God, I pause before I work-play
  to acknowledge you
  in the glory of your permanence.
You last
  through every generation
  and throughout eternity:
  always the same,
  never changing,
  in every season.

Pause to reflect

→

What contrast with the fabrics
*   that deploy my fingers and thoughts –*
*   so fragile,*
*   so prone to spoil,*
*   fray,*
*   decay.*
I could grieve that all I create is
*   destined to fade!*
But – and this is what I choose to do –
*   I could pray*
*   that something might yet remain:*
*   some impact,*
*   some influence,*
*   a memory of deep significance.*
Let my hands-on craft
*   have a hands-off quality,*
*   a yielding,*
*   an offering*
*   to you, holy God.*
Do with it, with me,
*   what you will*
*   for your sake.*
Amen.

———

God, as I picked up my work where I left off yesterday,
  I found none of the beauty I remembered
  and my heart sank.
Instead, I noticed each glaring flaw:
  the skipped stitches, imperfectly placed;
  the unevenness in tension;
  the appearance of carelessness,
  despite taking such care!
Disappointment landed heavily,
  robbing me of hard-won joy.
For a moment, I flung it aside,
  wanting nothing more to do with it;
  then your word broke through:
  'Because of the Lord's great love we are not consumed.'

Pause to reflect

→

It is true that I cannot meet my own standards,
  that I am not a machine,
  nor am I perfect.
But you accept me as I am;
  my mistakes do not define me
  nor confine me.
So hold me fast as I unpick and rework,
  ever mindful of the infinite care you take with me.
Show me what matters and what does not,
  and lead me towards greater heights of beauty,
  deeper heart-satisfaction,
  and all-pervading peace.
Amen.

_____

Prayers for woodworkers

The righteous will flourish like a palm tree, they will grow like a cedar of Lebanon.

PSALM 92:12

So make yourself an ark of cypress wood; make rooms in it and coat it with pitch inside and out… But I will establish my covenant with you, and you will enter the ark – you and your sons and your wife and your sons' wives with you.

GENESIS 6:14, 18

Now Hiram king of Tyre sent envoys to David, along with cedar logs and carpenters and stonemasons, and they built a palace for David.

2 SAMUEL 5:11

God, what glory is seen in the trees!
How they reveal your very nature:
  their rootedness,
  their protective canopies,
  their capacity for blossom and fruit
  all speaking of you.
Let my own roots grow
  deep down into your love,
  so I can stand tall when storms come
  and have no fear when life is dry.

Pause to reflect

→

But God…
Did you know how beautiful they were
  inside – hidden away –
  waiting for the moment
  when an axe or hurricane
  caused one to topple?
Each ring a testimony to life,
  each knot a scar;
  and the grain –
  oh, the grain! –
  that shouts gloriously,
    'I am not just tree!
    I am oak,
    I am yew,
    I am…'
Truly, at my bench today,
  I am on sacred ground,
  in awe of you, God,
  and your astonishing creation.
Amen.

———

God, I thank you for my skills
  passed down from generation to generation,
  as Joseph did for Jesus.
I handle with utmost respect
  and deep gratitude
  the tools which bear the sweat and oil
  of my forebears.
Sharpen my senses today
  as surely as I sharpen my tools.
Let me have eyes that see clearly
  the way the grain is running,
  so my cuts are sympathetic,
  harmonious.
Keep my hands from slipping –
  protect me, Lord,
  as well as this wood!
Help me let go of my crippling perfectionism
  and let the wood teach me
  what it is to let flaws
  speak a better word.
Together:
  you, me and this material of your creation,
  let us bring forth new beauty
  that glorifies you.
Amen.

_____

God, I've been so aware of you
  and your life lessons
  as I've worked on this piece.
How you found me in my raw state,
  felled by circumstances,
  my fruiting days over.
When you had to chop out what was spoiling me,
  your chisel did not slip;
  your focus did not wander.
You worked and you worked
  until, gradually, gradually,
  what you could see all along
  began to reveal itself to the world.
I am still a work in progress.
There are times you still need to apply your hand,
  sanding away my hard edges,
  gripping me tight so I neither warp nor twist.
Then you send your Holy Spirit,
  glorious comforter and healer,
  to polish and smooth and caress
  so gently that all else fades away.
I understand this about wood.
Do I understand it about me?
Teach me, Lord,
  I have so much still to learn.
Amen.

———

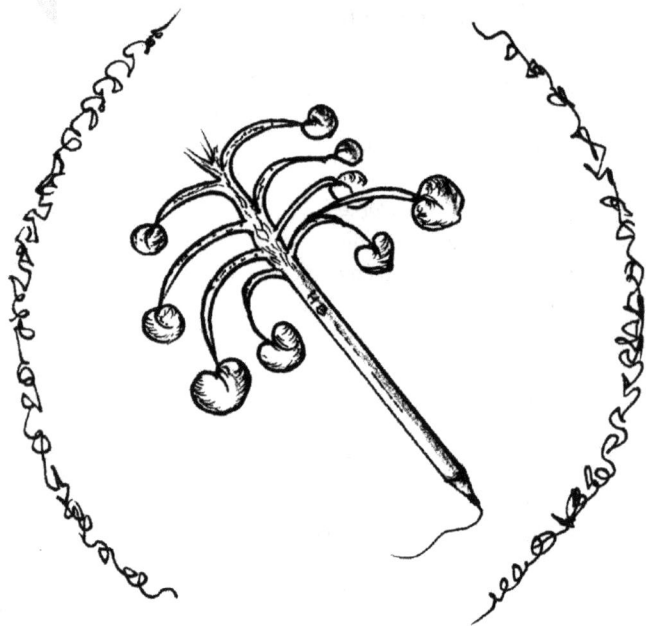

Prayers for writers/ poets/spoken-word artists/script-writers

My heart is stirred by a noble theme as I recite my verses for the king; my tongue is the pen of a skilful writer.
PSALM 45:1

And I saw six men coming from the direction of the upper gate, which faces north, each with a deadly weapon in his hand. With them was a man clothed in linen who had a writing kit at his side. They came in and stood beside the bronze altar.
EZEKIEL 9:2

'This is what the Lord, the God of Israel, says: "Write in a book all the words I have spoken to you."'
JEREMIAH 30:2

God, thank you for calling me to be a writer.
Thank you for the fun of playing with words,
relishing the feel of them on my tongue
as I commit them to the page.
Thank you for the way my mind works –
a mystery to all but you!
Thank you for the sense of creating raw material
that I can then mould and shape
through the wonderful, grace-filled gift of editing.
I don't take this responsibility lightly.
I receive this calling as an honour
and pray for more anointing today
to out-work it.
Let me handle each word carefully,
position each one precisely,
treating them as the precious treasure they are.
Amen.

―――

God, I sit with the blank screen/page
  in front of me,
  waiting,
  breath held.
In the silence, I pause,
  half-expecting the usual inner monologue –
  attributed to the page
  but entirely coming from me:
  the taunts,
  the reminders of past days
  when words have not flowed
  or, if they have, they were poor ones.
Today the anticipation is a peaceful one.
In the emptiness I see
  opportunity,
  not threat.
I see freedom
  as I set my mind to focus.
Soon, as Wordsworth said,
  the white space will be filled with
  the 'breathings of my heart'.
Yielded to you,
  steady in my soul,
  I can begin.
Amen.

———

God, I have been content
for you to be
my audience of one.
I have written and crafted
with your eyes ever on me,
sensing your pleasure
and your correction.
But my heart is restless
as I write today,
longing for others to read and hear
what I believe is worth sharing.
I need readers, Lord;
I need an audience.
I need to know that I am not just talking to myself
but to others – many, many others – too.
Can you help me find them?
Give me courage, I pray,
to risk rejection
and offer all you have given me.
Let me dare make those tentative steps
beyond my four walls
and into someone else's world.
Amen.

_____

God, I want to bring before you
  the pain of rejection.
You know how hard I have worked,
  how much I had committed it all to you,
  and it's unbearable to have it knocked back.
Come close to me as I mourn,
  regroup,
    reassess.
Help me not to let that word 'no'
  prevent me from trying again.
Help me trust that you will open up
  fresh opportunities,
  in different – better – directions,
  and help me not be envious of those who are succeeding.
I believe you hear and answer my prayers,
  and on your goodness I depend.
Amen.

———

Epilogue

Great are the works of the Lord; they are pondered by all who delight in them.

PSALM 111:2

Whatever you do, work at it with all your heart, as working for the Lord, not for human masters, since you know that you will receive an inheritance from the Lord as a reward. It is the Lord Christ you are serving.

COLOSSIANS 3:23–24

… being confident of this, that he who began a good work in you will carry it on to completion until the day of Christ Jesus.

PHILIPPIANS 1:6

Engaging with God in prayer is never meant to be a case of 'pushing a button and getting something out'. Instead, it's an expression of our relationship with him, which includes his delightful invitation for us to partner with him in his creativity.

Nor is it a 'say it once and move on' experience. The Bible talks about praying with perseverance (e.g. Ephesians 6:18) and, much as this can be frustrating for us, it's another opportunity to deepen our connection with God. As creatives, we understand the value of taking our time, not rushing the process. So it is with prayer.

My ongoing prayer is that, as we continue to seek God in our creative endeavours, we would not only produce works of great beauty and merit but would witness transformation in our lives. It's something of a cliché that we are all 'works in progress', but it's no less true for all that. God is constantly at work in us, shaping and polishing us – sometimes with pain in the process – to demonstrate his glory. He never settles back and says, 'That will do.' We are *so* much more valuable than that!

I hope that you will find yourself turning to this book again and again. (May it become dog-eared in the Lord's service!) I hope, too, that you will be inspired to compose your own prayers. Write them before praying, or as a record of what you hear yourself saying. I don't doubt they will be surprising as well as inspiring.

Above all, take heart.

Work-play as if it all depends on you.

Pray as if it all depends on God.

May the beauty of Jesus be seen in all we do and all we become.

Acknowledgements

In reflecting on a lifetime love of all things creative, I want to honour the people in my life who have taught, encouraged, and equipped me, as well as helping me raise my game. My parents, who made space and gave opportunity for my pursuits (and for making me left-handed, which I've always cherished!) My music teachers Margaret Jewell and Rex Ayling, who fostered a love for not just playing but also teaching. My family, for their constant love and their own creativity, which blesses me more than I can say.

In writing this book, I want to thank the Association of Christian Writers, who collectively have always inspired me to reach higher, further, and deeper. My two writing groups: Brecks, Fens and Pens, and Green Pastures Christian Writers, have been particularly encouraging on a personal level.

I extend huge thanks to the BRF Ministries team who have turned my raw manuscript into gold. I'm grateful to you all.

I owe a debt of thanks to my beloved husband, Roy, who is endlessly patient with my 'crafting mess' and superbly supportive in all I do. You are God's precious gift to me. I couldn't do any of this without you.

Lastly, and underpinning all that I am, my heart's gratitude to my loving creator God, who alone does all things well.

Index

BRF Ministries

Inspiring people of all ages to grow in Christian faith

BRF Ministries is the
home of Anna Chaplaincy,
BRF Resources, Messy Church
and Parenting for Faith

As a charity, our work would not be possible without fundraising and gifts in wills.
To find out more and to donate,
visit brf.org.uk/give or call +44 (0)1865 319700

Registered with
FUNDRAISING
REGULATOR

www.ingramcontent.com/pod-product-compliance
Lightning Source LLC
Chambersburg PA
CBHW051414090426
42737CB00014B/2666